GERMAN
GCSE Grade Booster

C. A. Willey

Schofield & Sims Ltd.

© 1991 Schofield & Sims Ltd.

All rights reserved.
No part of this publication may be
reproduced, stored in a retrieval system, or
transmitted, in any form, or by any means,
electronic, mechanical, photocopying,
recording or otherwise, without the prior
permission of Schofield & Sims Ltd.

0 7217 4618 7

First printed 1991

Schofield & Sims Ltd.
Dogley Mill
Fenay Bridge
Huddersfield
HD8 0NQ
England

Typeset by Ocean, Leeds
Printed in Great Britain by the Alden Press, Oxford

Contents

Introduction	5
1 Self and Family	7
2 House and Home	14
3 Town and Country	22
4 Buying and Selling	29
5 Food and Drink	39
6 School and Work	48
7 Sport and Leisure	56
8 Holidays and Travel	64
9 Services and Emergencies	73
10 Health and Welfare	82
Grammar	88
Examination Technique and Useful Tips	107
Reading Tests	114
Listening Tests	124
Answers to Reading and Listening Tests	126

Acknowledgements

The author and the publishers wish to thank the following for permission to use copyright material:

Bergsteigerschule, Kandersteg: p.8

Jugendscala: pp.23, 25, 33, 43, 49, 50, 51, 57, 59, 115, 118, 121, 122

Northern Examining Association (Yorkshire & Humberside Regional Examinations Board): pp.41, 52

Deutsche Bundesbahn: pp.68, 69, 123

Keimer Verlag: p.109

Introduction

Using the Book

This GCSE Grade Booster aims to give you the means and the confidence to achieve effective communication in German. It will help you to develop and practise the four skills tested by the GCSE examination – Reading, Writing, Speaking and Listening. The book contains the topic material required by most GCSE syllabuses, and provides wide coverage of the essential core material which needs to be mastered in order to achieve a good grade.

The syllabus content is covered in ten Topic Units. The first part of each Unit sets out essential information on the topic concerned, giving details of what you are required to know for the examination. The second part is devoted to practising the four skills through a selection of examination-type questions, to which specimen answers are given where appropriate. Vocabulary and idioms are supplied to aid understanding. As the Topic Units present varying degrees of difficulty, the Skills Practice sections also reflect these variations, and as much variety as possible has been included.

After the ten Topic Units comes a useful chapter on grammar. In a book of this size it is not possible or practical to provide a full revision course of German grammar. Instead, the particular difficulties which many students experience when faced with grammar in examination questions have been highlighted and explained in some detail, with examples in German and in English. This is followed by a chapter on examination technique. Finally, there is a chapter of sample Reading Tests and a chapter consisting of questions for the Listening Tests which are on the tape, Answers are also given for these.

Using the Tape

Some of the German material is recorded on the accompanying tape for Listening practice and some can be found both on the tape and in the book (some appears only in the book, for Reading practice). At the beginning of the tape you will hear a brief general introduction. Most of the Speaking exercises are recorded on the tape for you to check your answers against. Where the role-play is less structured, i.e. where you are asked to develop both sides of a conversation, a specimen conversation has been provided for guidance and practice.

Using the Tape

Speaking Practice

These exercises mostly take the form of a role-play or an interview. Read the introduction to the exercise in question and then study the actual role-play or interview. Prepare your responses and switch on the cassette. At the beginning of each Speaking exercise a linking voice will give details of what you are going to hear, so that you know exactly where you are, e.g. "Unit 3, page 22, Speaking Practice – Answers to Role-play exercise". The role-play then follows.
Remember:
- Prepare your part *before* switching on the cassette, to avoid hesitations.
- It is important to say the dialogue *out loud*.
- Switch off the cassette if you need more time to say your line. Don't gabble your words in a rush or let yourself be cut off half-way through.

Listening Practice

With the book open at the appropriate page, read the short introductory passage to the Listening exercise you wish to attempt. Now switch on the cassette. Each Listening exercise on the tape is preceded by details of what you will hear, e.g. "Unit 2, page 20, Listening Practice – The Removal (Der Umzug). Here is a conversation . . ." The dialogue then follows. At the end of the conversation the linking voice will say "Now answer the questions on page . . .". This refers to the sections in the book headed "Test Your Understanding". The answers to the questions are printed in the book.

1 Self and Family

Who Am I?

This is a short but vital unit which is directly personal and is therefore the starting-point for all the other units. In the exam, you will be required to talk and write about yourself, your family and your friends. You should be able to respond confidently in interviews, on the telephone or when filling in forms. Here are the elements of identification:

- Name (be able to spell it using the German alphabet)
- Address and phone number
- Age and birthday
- Nationality
- Status (married or single)
- Religion
- Occupation
- Details of physical appearance
- Qualities of character and disposition.

If you have to provide information about yourself, it will often be in response to such questions as:

- *Wie heißt du?   Wie ist dein Name?*
- *Wo wohnst du?   Was ist deine Adresse?*
- *Woher kommst du?   Wo bist du geboren?*
- *Wie alt bist du?   Wann bist du geboren?*
- *Wann hast du Geburtstag?*
- *Gehst du noch zur Schule?*
- *Was bist du von Beruf?   Was willst du werden?*
- Remember that if you are asked the question *Hast du Geschwister?* you are being asked if you have any brothers and sisters. If, for instance, you have one brother, the answer will be: *Ja, ich habe einen Bruder.*

Speaking Practice

1. Either on your own, or preferably with a partner, ask and answer in German the questions suggested above.

2. Reword the above questions so that they refer to someone else – your brother, sister or friend. For example, the first question becomes: *Wie heißt er?* or *Wie heißt sie? Wie ist sein Name?* or *Wie ist ihr Name?* Then answer the new set of questions about that person, for example: *Er heißt Brian* or *Sein Name ist Brian.*

Writing Practice

1. The daughter of your mother's long-standing German pen-friend is coming to work in England and will live with your family for a year. To help her get to know your family, you send her a family tree accompanied by a short description of each of six members of the family – e.g. brother, aunt, cousin, grandmother, etc. – along the following lines:

Onkel Stanley: Er ist groß und dünn und hat einen Schnurrbart. Er ißt kein Fleisch und er lacht viel. Er hat eine Gemüsehandlung und er arbeitet fleißig in seinem Laden.

2. Fill in this form applying for a place on a beginners' course in mountaineering.

Anmeldung

an die Schweizerische Bergsteigerschule Schwarenbach
CH-3718 **Kandersteg**

Der / die Unterzeichnete

Name: _____

Vorname: _____

Geburtsjahr: _____

Beruf: _____

Wohnort: _____

Adresse: _____

Tel.-Nr.: _____

meldet sich hiermit an zur Teilnahme

am Anfängerkurs	Nr. _1_	vom _6. Juli_	bis _12. Juli_
am Fortg.-Kurs	Nr. _____	vom _____	bis _____
an der Tourenwoche	Nr. _____	vom _____	bis _____
am Wochenendkurs	Nr. _____	vom _____	

an der geführten Bergtour vom _____

Datum: _____

Unterschrift: _____

3. You are looking for a new pen-friend and want to be properly matched up to a suitable boy. Write a short letter introducing yourself and describing your family and your interests.

Specimen Answer

> Halifax den 23. März
>
> Lieber Brieffreund,
>
> Ich heiße Sarah und ich bin 14 Jahre alt. Ich habe am 4. Januar Geburtstag. Ich suche einen Brieffreund in Deutschland. Ich habe zwei Brüder aber keine Schwester und ich habe einen kleinen weißen Hund. Er heißt Slipper. Mein Vater arbeitet für eine große Firma und fährt viel mit dem Auto. Meine Mutter arbeitet zu Hause. Wir wohnen in einem Doppelhaus in Halifax. Halifax ist eine große Stadt in Nordengland. In meiner Freizeit treibe ich Sport. Ich spiele gern Tennis und gehe auch oft schwimmen. Schreib mir bitte bald.
>
> Deine Sarah

Reading Practice

This section introduces Karen and Karl-Heinz, who first meet and become friends whilst on holiday in Yugoslavia. Their dialogue is divided into three parts, all of which are printed in the book. Parts 2 and 3 are also on the tape, so they may be used for either Listening or Reading practice. Useful vocabulary is provided for all three conversations.

Read this first conversation between Karen and Karl-Heinz when they meet in the café on a camp-site in Yugoslavia.

KARL-HEINZ: Darf ich mich zu Ihnen setzen?
KAREN: Ja, sicher, wir sind hier zu dritt; der vierte Platz ist also frei. Meine Freundinnen holen uns etwas zu essen, während ich den Tisch frei halte.
KARL-HEINZ: Ist es hier immer so voll?

KAREN:	Um diese Zeit, ja. Alle wollen gegen Mittag essen. Es ist dann zu heiß in der Sonne, und man hat eine bessere Auswahl, wenn man vor ein Uhr ißt.
KARL-HEINZ:	Wie lange sind Sie schon hier?
KAREN:	Seit einer Woche. Wir haben einen Wohnwagen gemietet.
KARL-HEINZ:	Wie gefällt es Ihnen hier?
KAREN:	Sehr gut. Wir verlangen nicht viel, nur Sonne, See und Spaß, und das alles haben wir hier gefunden.
KARL-HEINZ:	Ich bin eben erst angekommen. Mein Freund Johann und ich wollen ein paar Tage hier zelten. Vielleicht können Sie uns Auskunft geben über diesen Ort, wo wir am besten essen können, wo man Reiseschecks einlösen kann, usw.

(Jenny und Sarah kommen mit dem Essen zum Tisch)

KAREN:	Jenny and Sarah, this is – I'm sorry. Ich weiß ja noch nicht, wie Sie heißen.
KARL-HEINZ:	Sagen wir bitte du. Wir sind doch alle ungefähr im gleichen Alter. Darf ich mich vorstellen? Ich bin Karl-Heinz Kunert und ich komme aus Neustadt in der Nähe von Köln. Ich studiere an der Universität in Köln.
KAREN:	Ich bin Karen Mortimer und dies sind meine Freundinnen Jenny und Sarah. Nachdem wir gegessen haben, kann ich dich ein bißchen herumführen. Jenny und Sarah haben andere Pläne für den Nachmittag, daher habe ich Zeit.
KARL-HEINZ:	Abgemacht! Also, guten Appetit!

Vocabulary and Expressions

zu dritt as a threesome
gegen Mittag at about noon
die Auswahl (-en) choice, selection
der Wohnwagen (-) caravan
mieten to hire, to rent
verlangen to demand
der Spaß fun
eben erst only just

zelten to camp
Auskunft geben to tell, to inform
Reiseschecks einlösen to cash travellers' cheques
ungefähr approximately
im gleichen Alter the same age
sich vorstellen to introduce oneself
abgemacht! agreed!

Test Your Understanding

Answer these questions in English.
1. Where are Karen's friends when Karl-Heinz arrives?
2. Give TWO reasons why the café is so full of people at this time.

3. Where are Karen and her friends staying?
4. What are their THREE holiday expectations?
5. What kind of information is Karl-Heinz looking for about this holiday spot?

Answers
1. Getting something to eat. 2. It's too hot in the sun and there's a better choice if you eat before one o'clock. 3 In a caravan. 4. Sun, sea and fun. 5. He wants to know about good places to eat and where to change travellers' cheques.

Listening or Reading Practice

Now listen to or read the second conversation between Karen and Karl-Heinz, which takes place outside a café in the town.

KAREN: Ich komme aus Moortown in Yorkshire und mache nächstes Jahr das Abitur, das heißt, meine ,,A levels". Ich lerne gern Fremdsprachen und möchte Deutsch und Französisch studieren.
KARL-HEINZ: Du kannst sehr gut Deutsch sprechen. Warst du schon mal in Deutschland?
KAREN: Ja, ich war im Frühjahr auf einem Gymnasium dort. Ich habe drei Monate bei einer Familie gewohnt und ging mit der Tochter zur Schule. Es war toll, und ich habe viel Deutsch gelernt, da die Eltern kein Englisch konnten.
KARL-HEINZ: Wo war das eigentlich?
KAREN: In Hünfeld. Das ist eine Kleinstadt in Hessen.
KARL-HEINZ: Warst du schon in Köln oder irgendwo anders am Rhein?
KAREN: Nein, die Gegend kenne ich noch nicht, aber ich hoffe, nachdem ich mit der Schule fertig bin, und bevor ich auf die Uni gehe, ein Jahr in Deutschland zu verbringen. Ich hoffe, Arbeit zu finden und auch ein bißchen herumreisen zu können.
KARL-HEINZ: Was denkt deine Familie darüber?
KAREN: Sie wollen nur das Beste für mich und sind froh, daß ich so genau weiß, was ich machen will. Solange ich regelmäßig von mir hören lasse, entweder telefonisch oder schriftlich, machen sie sich keine Sorgen.
KARL-HEINZ: Das erinnert mich eben daran, daß ich zu Hause anrufen muß, um Bescheid zu sagen, daß Johann und ich sicher angekommen sind und einen Campingplatz gefunden haben.

Vocabulary and Expressions

die Fremdsprache (-n) foreign language	sich Sorgen machen to be worried
das Frühjahr spring	erinnern to remind
toll great, terrific	das erinnert mich daran, daß . . . that reminds me that . . .
regelmäßig regular	
entweder . . . oder either . . . or	Bescheid sagen to say, to inform
schriftlich in writing	sicher safe

Test Your Understanding
Answer these questions in English.
1. What are Karen's study plans for the future?
2. Where did Karen spend last spring term?
3. What do you learn about the parents in the German family she stayed with?
4. What is Karen hoping to do between leaving school and going to university?
5. How does she make sure her parents need not worry about her?

Answers
1. She wants to study German and French. 2. At a grammar school in Germany. 3. They could not speak English. 4. She wants to spend a year in Germany, working and travelling around. 5. By phoning or writing regularly.

Additional Listening or Reading Practice

Now listen to or read the third conversation, which Karen and Karl-Heinz have as they walk back to the camp-site.

KAREN: Bist du ein Einzelkind?
KARL-HEINZ: Leider nicht! Aber so schlimm sind meine Geschwister auch nicht. Ich habe zwei ältere Schwestern, Hannelore und Wiebke, und einen jüngeren Bruder, Georg.
KAREN: Wie alt sind sie?
KARL-HEINZ: Hannelore und Wiebke sind fünfundzwanzig; sie sind nämlich Zwillinge. Georg wird wohl vierzehn Jahre alt sein.
KAREN: Haben sie auch braune Haare und braune Augen, wie du?
KARL-HEINZ: Keineswegs. Meine Mutter hat blondes Haar und blaue Augen, die Zwillinge und Georg auch. Hannelore hat lockiges Haar und Wiebke glattes Haar, aber sonst sind sie sich sehr ähnlich, die Zwillinge.

Additional Listening or Reading Practice

KAREN: Kommst du gut mit ihnen aus?
KARL-HEINZ: Mit meinen Schwestern schon, besonders seit sie nicht mehr bei uns zu Hause wohnen. Außerdem ist Hannelore verheiratet. Mit Georg ist es aber ein bißchen anders. Ich wohne noch zu Hause und muß viel studieren. Er bringt seine lauten Kameraden nach Hause und sie hören sich Platten an und machen überhaupt viel Lärm und Unordnung. Als jüngstes Kind ist er etwas verwöhnt und kann lästig sein. Ich war sicherlich nicht so doof und frech, als ich in seinem Alter war.
KAREN: Nein, du warst immer fleißig und schüchtern, hattest Angst vor deinen Schwestern und warst überhaupt ein Musterkind, nicht wahr?

Vocabulary and Expressions

das Einzelkind (-er) only child	**die Unordnung** untidiness
der Zwilling (-e) twin	**verwöhnt** spoilt
keineswegs not at all	**lästig sein** to be a nuisance
lockig curly	**sicherlich** certainly
glatt straight, smooth	**doof** stupid
ähnlich similar, alike	**frech** cheeky
gut mit ihm auskommen to get on well with him	**fleißig** hard-working
	schüchtern shy
außerdem besides	**überhaupt** altogether
verheiratet married	**das Musterkind (-er)** model child
der Lärm noise	

Test Your Understanding

Answer these questions in English.
1. How many brothers and sisters has Karl-Heinz?
2. What is special about his sisters?
3. How can you easily tell his sisters apart?
4. What annoys Karl-Heinz about his brother Georg?
5. In which THREE ways does Karen jokingly suggest that Karl-Heinz must have been a model child?

Answers

1. 3 – 2 sisters, 1 brother. 2. They are twins. 3. One has curly hair, one has straight hair. 4. He is noisy and untidy, especially when he brings his friends to the house. 5. She suggests he was hard-working, shy and afraid of his sisters.

2 House and Home

Where Do You Live?

This topic, concerning the home and its normal routines, covers a number of different areas. You should be able to talk and write about all of the topics which follow.

House

Houses and flats of all kinds, the rooms, including attic and cellar where necessary, and also the garden and garage. Here is a plan of a flat. Make sure you know the names of all the rooms.

das WOHNZIMMER (living-room)	das SCHLAFZIMMER (bedroom)	das ARBEITSZIMMER (study)
	der FLUR (hall)	
das ESSZIMMER (dining-room)	die KÜCHE (kitchen) / das BADEZIMMER (bathroom)	das SCHLAFZIMMER (bedroom)
der BALKON (balcony)		

Household

Members of the household, family and pets.

Rooms

Size, shape, furniture, decoration and location. Say if you have your own room and describe it or the room where you sleep.

Location

Your local area and its amenities, where things and places are, firstly the house itself, and then, more particularly, where rooms and various articles are to be found in the house, garden or garage.

Hospitality

The needs of a guest, e.g. food, drink, bathroom, toilet, bedroom, soap, towel. Also be able to ask for all these things as a guest yourself.

Daily Routine
Daily and weekly patterns of activity and behaviour which take place in and around the house, e.g.:
- Getting up
- Going to bed
- Preparing meals, eating and clearing up afterwards
- Cleaning and tidying the house
- Washing the car
- Gardening

Special Occasions
There are many special occasions celebrated in the home which you should be able to discuss and describe – for example, birthdays, weddings, Christmas, Easter, family get-togethers, parties, etc.

Speaking Practice
The answers to these Speaking exercises are on the tape.

Role-play 1
You have just arrived at your German pen-friend's house for a fortnight's visit and your pen-friend's mother is trying to find out how you are feeling and what you need.
a) (How was the journey?)
   Say it was long but interesting.
b) (Are you tired? Would you like to go to bed?)
   Say yes, you are tired, but you do not want to go to bed yet.
c) (Are you hungry or thirsty?)
   Say you would like something to drink, but you are not hungry.
d) (Shall I show you your room?)
   Say yes please, and ask where the bathroom and toilet are.

Role-play 2
Dorle is moving out of the bedroom she used to share with her sister into the room vacated by her recently married brother. She and her mother are discussing the conversion of the room into a study-bedroom. Develop the conversation, using *some* of the following points as guide-lines:
a) How the room has become available and how Dorle would like to use it.
b) The arrangement of the furniture, bed, desk, cupboards, chest of drawers, etc.

c) Dorle would like a white carpet and her mother objects, giving reasons and suggesting a more practical colour.
d) Dorle points out the advantages of having her own study-bedroom and her mother tries to make her aware that there are responsibilities, too, such as keeping it clean and tidy.

Reading Practice

1. Read the following description of the Kunerts' living-room. Helpful vocabulary is provided.

Es hat bequeme Sitzmöbel. Die Kunerts sitzen hier gern in ihrer Freizeit zusammen. Sie spielen dann Karten, sehen fern oder unterhalten sich. Oft ist Besuch da. Die Schrankwand ist eine Kombination aus mehreren Schränken: Schränke für Gläser, Flaschen, Besteck, Geschirr, Tischwäsche und Bücher. Vor dem Fenster stehen das Farbfernsehgerät, ein Schallplattenschrank mit einer Stereoanlage und eine grüne Zimmerpalme. Rechts hinten steht ein Schreibtisch, wo Frau Kunert ihre Briefe schreibt. Vor dem Sofa steht ein langer Tisch. Jeden Sonntagnachmittag sitzt die Familie zum Kaffeetrinken zusammen um den Tisch. Auf dem Fußboden liegt ein moderner Teppich aus Wolle in verschiedenen Farben. Ein Bild in lebhaften Farben hängt an der Wand links. Die Kunerts lieben Zimmerpflanzen. Deshalb stehen Blumentöpfe auf dem Fensterbrett.

Vocabulary and Expressions

bequem comfortable
die Sitzmöbel (pl.) furniture for sitting on
sich unterhalten to talk together
die Schrankwand (¨e) wall of cupboards, units
das Besteck (-e) cutlery
das Geschirr crockery
die Tischwäsche table linen
das Farbfernsehgerät (-e) colour television set

der Schallplattenschrank (¨e) record cabinet
die Stereoanlage (-n) stereo unit
die Zimmerpalme (-n) a kind of house-plant
der Teppich (-e) carpet
die Wolle wool
verschieden various, different
lebhaft lively, bright
der Blumentopf (¨e) plant pot
das Fensterbrett (-er) window-ledge

Test Your Understanding

Answer these questions in English.
a) Name THREE of the Kunerts' leisure activities.
b) List SIX items to be found in the wall cupboards.

Reading Practice

c) Name TWO things to be found in front of the window.
d) What is on the right at the back of the room and who uses it for what purpose?
e) What do the Kunerts do on Sunday afternoons?
f) Describe the carpet.
g) What can be seen on the window ledge?

Answers

a) Playing cards, watching television, talking. b) Glasses, bottles, cutlery, crockery, table linen, books. c) 2 of: colour television set, record cabinet with stereo unit, house-plant. d) A writing desk where Frau Kunert writes letters. e) They have coffee together. f) It is modern, made of wool and of various colours. g) Plant pots.

2. Louise receives a letter from her new German pen-friend, Dagmar, and writes back to her. You will find out more about who Louise and Dagmar are by reading their letters. Here is Dagmar's letter to Louise. Helpful vocabulary is provided on page 18.

Neustadt, den 25. August

Liebe Louise

Es freut mich, daß ich endlich eine englische Brieffreundin habe. Willst Du mir bitte in Deinem nächsten Brief etwas mehr über Deine Familie und Euer Haus schreiben? Hast Du ein Haustier? Kommst Du gut mit Deinen Geschwistern aus? Deine Schwester Karen ist sehr nett, finde ich. Sie war gestern bei uns und hat mir Deinen Brief gegeben. Mein älterer Bruder Johann kennt ihren Freund Karl-Heinz von der Schule her.

Johann geht jetzt auf die Uni. Er studiert Physik und Chemie und ist sehr gescheit (das muß ich zugeben, obwohl er mein Bruder ist!). Mein anderer Bruder Peter geht noch zur Schule, denn er ist erst zwölf Jahre alt. Ich bin 15 und habe am 20. September Geburtstag. Ich interessiere mich für vieles, für Sport, Musik (Popmusik und klassische Musik), Fremdsprachen, lesen und Fotographieren. Ich kann ein bißchen Geige spielen und gehe jede Woche zum Turnverein.

Das wäre es für heute, weil ich gleich zum Turnverein muß. Hoffentlich werde ich bald von Dir hören!

Deine Dagmar

Reading Practice

Vocabulary and Expressions

es freut mich I am pleased
der Brieffreund (-e)/die Brieffreundin (-nen) pen-friend
auf die Uni(versität) gehen to go to university
gescheit clever
zugeben to admit
obwohl although
sich interessieren für to be interested in
die Fremdsprache (-n) foreign language
Geige spielen to play the violin
der Turnverein (-e) gym club

Test Your Understanding

Answer these questions in English.
a) How did Dagmar become Louise's pen-friend?
b) What do you find out about Dagmar's brothers?
c) What are Dagmar's interests, apart from sport and music?
d) Which musical instrument does she play?
e) What is her main sporting interest?

Answers

a) Dagmar's elder brother knows Karl-Heinz; Karen and Karl-Heinz visited Dagmar's family and Karen gave Dagmar Louise's letter. b) Johann is studying Physics and Chemistry at university; he is very clever. Peter is 12 and is still at school. c) Foreign languages, reading, photography. d) The violin. e) Gymnastics.

3. Now read Louise's reply to Dagmar, using the vocabulary to help you.

Moortown, den 7. September

Liebe Dagmar,

Vielen Dank für Deinen netten Brief. Es freut mich auch, daß ich eine neue Brieffreundin habe, an die ich auf Deutsch schreiben kann. Ich lerne seit zwei Jahren in der Schule Deutsch. Meine Lieblingsfächer sind jedoch Mathe und Physik und ich möchte Medizin studieren, wenn meine Noten beim Abitur gut genug sind.

Ich habe auch einen älteren Bruder; er heißt Robert. Er ist 24 Jahre alt und ist verheiratet. Seine Frau heißt Sandra und sie erwartet ein Kind. Wir freuen uns alle so sehr auf das neue Baby! Meine Mutter ist Schulsekretärin und mein Vater ist Manager von einem kleinen Supermarkt.

> Wir wohnen in einem ziemlich alten Einfamilienhaus
> in Moortown. Ich habe mein eigenes Schlafzimmer
> unter dem Dach. Es ist klein und hat schiefe Wände,
> aber ich kann dort ungestört meine Schallplatten
> hören und auch die Wände mit Bildern und
> Plakaten bekleben.
> Ich habe zwei Katzen, Flotsam und Jetsam. Jetsam
> gehört eigentlich meinem Bruder, aber er hat sie
> mir geschenkt, als er Sandra heiratete.
> Ich komme meistens gut aus mit Robert und
> Karen, besser als früher, als wir jünger waren.
> Erzähle mir noch etwas über Deine Familie und über
> Neustadt und schicke mir bitte ein Bild von Dir.
> Ich lege zwei Bilder bei, eins von mir und eins von
> den Katzen. Hoffentlich geht es Dir und Deiner Familie gut.
>   Tschüß!   Deine Louise

Vocabulary and Expressions

das Lieblingsfach (¨-er) favourite subject
verheiratet married
erwarten to expect
sich freuen auf + Acc. to look forward to
der Supermarkt (¨-e) supermarket
das Einfamilienhaus (¨-er) detached house
das Dach (¨-er) roof

schief sloping
die Wand (¨-e) wall
die Schallplatte (-n) record
ungestört undisturbed
das Plakat (-e) poster
bekleben to cover, to stick on
mit jemandem gut auskommen to get on well with someone
beilegen to enclose

Test Your Understanding

Answer these questions in English.
a) What are Louise's favourite school subjects?
b) What do you find out about Louise's elder brother?
c) Give THREE facts about Louise's bedroom.
d) How does Louise get on with her brother and sister?
e) What does Louise send with her letter?

Answers

a) Maths and physics. b) He is called Robert, is 24 and married; He is about to become a father. c) It is under the roof, small and has sloping walls. d) Better now than she used to when they were all younger. e) 2 pictures – 1 of herself, 1 of her cats.

Writing Practice

1. Write your own letter of reply in German to Dagmar's letter. Include the following:
a) a suitable beginning and ending;
b) reasons why you are pleased to have a German pen-friend;
c) a brief description of your family;
d) brief details about where you live and a description of your bedroom;
e) some information about your pet(s);
f) some questions about herself and her family.

2. Write a description in six short phrases of a flat, as though it were being offered for rent. Include the following information:
It is on the third floor;
two bedrooms, one with a washbasin;
a large living-room with a balcony;
a kitchen with cooker and fridge;
a bathroom with WC and shower.

Answer
Mietwohnung
im dritten Stock;
zwei Schlafzimmer, eins mit Waschbecken;
großes Wohnzimmer mit Balkon;
Küche mit Herd und Kühlschrank;
Badezimmer mit Toilette und Dusche

3. Using the description of the Kunerts' living-room on page 16 as a guide, write your own description of the living-room or lounge at home.

Listening Practice

The Removal (Der Umzug)
The Kunerts are visited by friends of theirs, the Ringers, who used to be neighbours, but who have recently moved house. Listen to their conversation about the removal on the cassette. Useful vocabulary is given below.

Vocabulary and Expressions

die Etagenwohnung (-en) flat	**die Decke (-n)** ceiling, cover, blanket
die Wohnfläche (-n) living area	
die Altbauwohnung (-en) old-style flat, flat in an old building	**Ecken und Winkel** nooks and crannies

Listening Practice

geräumig spacious	der Möbelwagen (-) removal van
die Vorstellung (-en) idea	laden to load
planen to plan	eingerichtet equipped
das Grundstück (-e) plot of land	erfahren to find out
hinterlassen (insep.) to leave (in a will)	die Spedition removal firm
	sich herausstellen to turn out
pflegeleicht easy to look after	der Vordersitz (-e) front seat
einziehen to move in	das Sprichwort (⸚er) proverb
klappen to work, to go	Ende gut, alles gut! all's well that ends well!
der Möbelpacker (-) removal man	

Test Your Understanding

Answer these questions in English.
1. Give FOUR features of older-style flats mentioned by Frau Ringer.
2. How did the Ringers come by the land on which they had their house built?
3. Why did the Ringers want a smaller dwelling?
4. When did they move into the new house?
5. Why did the Ringers have no difficulties about getting a cooked meal on their first night in their new home, but had problems with sleeping arrangements?
6. Why could they not find out what had happened to the removal van? Give TWO reasons.
7. What had happened to the removal van?
8. Where did the Ringers sleep that night?
9. What positive attitude did the Ringers take at the end of this trying time?
10. Listen to the different words used for 'you' in this conversation – *du*, *ihr*, *Sie*, etc. What does this tell you about the relationship between the Ringers and the Kunerts (including Karen)?

Answers

1. 4 of: high ceilings, double doors, many nooks and crannies, spacious, larger rooms. 2. Frau Ringer's father died and left them a small building plot. 3. Their children have grown up and moved on. 4. 3 weeks ago. 5. The new kitchen was well equipped, but they had no beds or bedding. 6. They could not get through to the removal firm outside office hours and they had no telephone of their own at that time, so the removal firm could not let them know. 7. It broke down and they had to wait for a replacement van to arrive and complete the move. 8. In the car. 9. They consoled themselves with the proverb: All's well that ends well! 10. The Ringers and Kunerts were neighbours who became good friends, therefore they address each other as *du* in the singular and *ihr* in the plural. As an English visitor, Karen uses the polite or formal form and addresses the Ringers as *Sie*.

… Out and About · Speaking Practice

3 Town and Country

Out and About

This unit deals with places – where they are, what they are like, how to find your way there, etc. You should be able to:
- describe your own locality, whether city, town, village or countryside;
- ask other people about where they live, and express opinions on the subject.
- In a wider context, you should be able to comment on parts of German-speaking countries you have visited or read about.

You should be able to:
- ask the way, whether you are on foot or using transport;
- give someone else directions;
- pin-point a place precisely, and give an exact description of the location, whether in urban or rural surroundings. This includes descriptions of buildings, the whereabouts of shops, public buildings, local amenities and transport – for example, libraries, sports centres, bus-stops and stations.

Speaking Practice

The answers to the role-play exercise are on the tape.

Role-play

You have just arrived in a strange town where you are visiting a friend. You ask directions to his/her address.
a) Excuse me, can you tell me the way to the Winzerstraße? (Go to the next set of traffic-lights and turn left into the market-place. There you will find a town plan).
b) Do you know the Winzerstraße? (I have been there once, but cannot tell you exactly how to get there).
c) I shall look for the town plan in the market-place. Thank you. Goodbye. (Goodbye and good luck!)

Blindekuh (Blind Man's Buff)

For this exercise you need a partner who knows your local area as well as you do.

Choose a destination – for example, the home of a mutual friend, a particular classroom at school, a cinema or a shop. Without revealing what it is, give your partner precise directions in German on how to get there. At the end, he/she must say where he/she is. To keep a check on each other, your partner could repeat the directions after you – correcting any mistakes you might have made!

Reading Practice
1. Read the following article about life in the country.

Zurück zur Natur

Wer müde ist vom Lärm der Städte, den zieht es „zurück zur Natur". Jedes Wochenende rollt die „Blechlawine" der Autos mit Städtern in die nahen Wälder. Hier ist die Luft noch rein, hier kann man stundenlang spazierengehen und sieht kaum einen anderen Menschen. Der Wald, der in jeder Jahreszeit ein anderes Gesicht hat, erinnert an Märchen aus Kindertagen. Wo früher die bösen Räuber hausten, kann man heute den Streß aus Büro und Fabrik vergessen und in Ruhe und Frieden „Mensch sein".
Die Menschen, die auf dem Land leben und arbeiten, genießen natürlich auch die frische Luft. Aber ein ewiger Urlaub ist ihr Leben bestimmt nicht. Sicher hat sich in der Landwirtschaft vieles geändert.
Ein Bauer ist heute ein Geschäftsmann wie jeder andere. Maschinen ersetzen die menschliche Arbeits-

Reading Practice

kraft. Die jungen Leute aus den Dörfern fahren in die nächsten Städte und suchen dort Arbeit. Viele fahren 40 und mehr Kilometer am Tag, um zu ihrem Arbeitsplatz zu kommen. Diese Leute nennt man ,,Pendler". Sie fahren täglich zwischen Wohnort und Arbeitsplatz hin und her. Das Leben auf dem Land ist auch heute noch nicht leicht. Manchmal muß man weit fahren bis zum nächsten Arzt oder Krankenhaus, bis zur Sekundarschule oder zur Berufsausbildung. Ein Warenhaus für größere Einkäufe gibt es nur in der nächsten Kleinstadt.

Schlaue Bauern haben entdeckt, daß die ,,Städter" nicht nur am Wochenende gern aufs Land fahren. Der ,,Urlaub auf dem Bauernhof" ist zur Zeit ganz groß in Mode. Viele Bauern vermieten heute Zimmer an Feriengäste. Besonders Familien mit Kindern machen gern Urlaub auf dem Land. Hier ist genug Platz für Kinder. Hier gibt es Hunde und Katzen zum Spielen, Pferde zum Reiten und genug Kühe für frische Milch. Das Essen ist gut und auch nicht teuer. Viele Deutsche entdecken nach 5 Jahren Urlaub in Mallorca die Schönheit des eigenen Landes.

Test Your Understanding

a) Try to find other simple ways of expressing in German the following words and phrases:

1. ein Auto
2. ein Städter
3. die nahen Wälder
4. rein
5. spazierengehen
6. ein Märchen
7. sicher
8. am Tag
9. ein Warenhaus
10. schlau
11. zur Zeit
12. Urlaub

Answers

1. ein Wagen. 2. jemand, der in der Stadt wohnt. 3. die Wälder, die in der Nähe sind. 4. sauber. 5. einen Spaziergang machen. 6. eine Geschichte, die nicht wahr ist. 7. gewiß. 8. jeden Tag, täglich. 9. ein Kaufhaus. 10. klug, gescheit. 11. jetzt. 12. Ferien.

b) At the end of the article, reasons are given for town people liking to visit the country for a farmhouse holiday. Summarise these reasons in English.

Answers

There is enough room for children; there are dogs and cats to play with, horses to ride and enough cows for fresh milk. The food is good and not expensive.

c) The middle section of the article deals with the problems of people who live in the country. What are the problems mentioned here?

Reading Practice

Answers

Machines have replaced men and there is unemployment. Young people have to look for work in the towns. Many people have to commute 40 or more kilometres to work. You may well have a long journey to the nearest doctor or hospital, secondary school or training centre. Shopping is also restricted.

2. The following article for reading comprehension has been chosen as an example of a document with some difficult sections which you do not need to understand fully in order to get the right answers (see section on examination technique, page 108).

Raus auf's Land!

Abendstimmung auf dem Land. Martina (18) und Peter (20) arbeiten bei ihren Schafen auf der Weide. Die beiden wohnen in Dexheim, einem Dorf in Rhein-Hessen. Bis nach Mainz sind es etwa 25 Kilometer. Also nahe genug, um mal ins Kino zu gehen, oder auch in ein Café.

Martina und Peter haben schon als Kinder auf dem Land gelebt. Aber dann zogen ihre Eltern mit ihnen in die Stadt.

Vor kurzer Zeit bekam Martina den kleinen Bauernhof, als ihre Großmutter starb. Das Haus hat nur drei Zimmer. Aber ein großer Garten gehört dazu, ein Schafstall und etwas Weideland.

Martina macht zur Zeit ihr Abitur. Peter macht eine Ausbildung als Gärtner. Beide müssen also jeden Tag in die Stadt fahren. Warum wohnen sie dann hier auf dem Land? ,,Ich bin froh, wenn ich abends hier draußen sein kann", sagt Peter. ,,Das Stadtleben ist übertrieben. Die Menschen dort haben zu hohe

Ansprüche. Und wenn die nicht erfüllt werden, sind sie unzufrieden."

Aber warum macht er seine Ausbildung nicht auf dem Land? Peter schüttelt den Kopf. „Das ist sehr schwierig. Hier gibt es nur Stellen bei Bauern oder Winzern. Aber wie die mit der Natur umgehen – das will ich auf keinen Fall lernen . . ."

Martina wäscht Schafswolle in einem großen Wasser-Bottich. „Wir bauen hier Getreide und Gemüse für uns und die Tiere an", erzählt sie. „Außer den Schafen haben wir noch ein paar Enten und Hühner. Aus der Schafsmilch mache ich Käse, und die Wolle färbe ich mit Pflanzenfarben. Eine alte Frau im Dorf hat mir das gezeigt."

Ein paar kleine Enten spazieren durchs Gras. Die Hühner kratzen auf der Erde vor dem Gewächshaus. „Als die Katastrophe von Tschernobyl geschah, waren wir sehr froh über unser Gewächshaus", erzählt Martina. „Die Schafsmilch war radioaktiv, aber das Gemüse aus dem Treibhaus war in Ordnung."

Peter glaubt nicht, daß viele Menschen auf solche Warnungen hören. „Für die anderen sind wir ,Alternative' und leben in einer anderen Welt. – Ich glaube, das stimmt sogar. Wenn man so lebt wie wir, dann sieht man vieles anders und mit mehr Abstand. Aber nur so kann man Dinge erkennen, die gefährlich für uns alle sind."

Test Your Understanding

Answer these questions in English.
a) What is the nearest city to where Martina and Peter now live?
b) Have they always lived in the country? Give details.
c) How did they acquire their little farm?
d) What is there apart from the farmhouse?
e) What are the main occupations of Martina and Peter apart from the farm?
f) What THREE kinds of animal do they have?
g) What does Martina use to make cheese?
h) How does she dye the wool?
i) When did the greenhouse prove really useful?
j) What do they grow in the greenhouse?

Answers

a) Mainz. b) They lived in the country when they were children but then their families moved into the town. c) Martina got the farm when her grandmother died. d) A large garden, a sheep shed and pasture land. e) Martina is studying for her final examination at school, the German equivalent to A levels. Peter is training to be a gardener. f) Sheep, ducks and chickens. g) Sheep's milk. h) With plant dyes. i) When the Chernobyl disaster occurred and there was radioactive fallout. j) Vegetables.

Writing Practice

The German extracts for Reading practice in this unit illustrate the advantages and disadvantages of life in the country. Write an account of what it is like to live in a town, including the following points:
a) The features of a town, its buildings, shops, offices, streets, etc.
b) Traffic and transport in the town.
c) Where people live and the type of accommodation – for example, in the centre or the suburbs, in a flat or a house.
d) Amenities and entertainment, such as sports facilities, cinemas, cafés, discos, etc.
e) Why some people prefer to live and work in a town.

Answers

a) Eine Stadt hat viele Straßen und Gebäude; es sind Wohnhäuser, große und kleine Geschäfte, Schulen, Bürogebäude, ein Rathaus, eine Polizeiwache, ein Marktplatz, ein Bahnhof und Kirchen.
b) Es ist viel Verkehr in der Stadt, z.B. Autos, Lieferwagen und Busse. Es gibt Verkehrsampeln an den Straßenkreuzungen und es gibt Bushaltestellen, wo die Leute auf die Busse warten. Viele Städte haben heutzutage eine Fußgängerzone, wo die Leute auf verkehrsfreien Straßen in Ruhe einkaufen können.
c) Die Stadtleute wohnen in Häusern oder Etagenwohnungen, einige in der Stadtmitte, wo es laut und schmutzig sein kann, andere am Stadtrand, in den Vororten, wo es ruhiger ist, und wo die Luft sauberer ist. Viele Leute in den Vororten müssen in die Stadt fahren, um zur Arbeit oder zur Schule zu kommen.
d) Es gibt vielerlei Unterhaltungsmöglichkeiten in der Stadt, z.B. ein Fußballstadion, ein Theater, Kinos, Discos, Kneipen, Cafés, Parks und Sportplätze.
e) Viele Leute wollen lieber in der Stadt wohnen als auf dem Lande, weil sie das laute, lebhafte Leben in der Stadt gern haben. Diese Leute wohnen am liebsten in der Nähe vom Arbeitsplatz und sie finden, daß das Stadtleben viel anzubieten hat.

Listening Practice

Town Life or Country Life? (Stadtleben oder Landleben?)

Karl-Heinz has a friend at university who lives in the country and has come to Cologne to study. This friend, Norbert, goes home at weekends and he invites Karl-Heinz and Karen to spend a Sunday at his parents' house. They go for a walk and discuss the pros and cons of living in the country, especially for young people. Listen to their conversation on the cassette, using the vocabulary on page 28 to help you.

Listening Practice

Vocabulary and Expressions

bis auf except for
das ist es gerade that's just what I mean
der Lärm noise
die Ameise (-n) ant
der Verkehr traffic
wo denkst du hin! what do you think!
hassen to hate, to detest
das Gedränge crowds, crush of people
die Jugendlichen (pl.) young people
begeistert keen
die Kneipe (-n) pub
regelmäßig regular(ly)
sich treffen to meet

auffallen to be conspicuous
unter der Lupe stehen to be closely watched
den Führerschein machen to get one's driving-licence
das Mofa (-s) moped
damit so that, in order that
unabhängig independent
lärmend noisy
der Glanz der Großstadt bright lights of the city
sobald as soon as
heiraten to marry
sich flüchten to flee, to take refuge
die Erholung relaxation
ändern to change

Test Your Understanding

Answer these questions in English.
1. What is the only thing Karl-Heinz can hear?
2. How does Karen describe the people in the city?
3. When does Karl-Heinz find it difficult to sleep?
4. How does Karen find town life?
5. What is the biggest problem for young people in the country and how do they solve it?
6. What kind of evening entertainment is there for the young people in Norbert's village?
7. Why do these young people not like the café?
8. How do they achieve some independence?
9. What does Karen claim happens a bit later in life to these young people who go into the towns?

Answers

1. The birds. 2. They run around like ants. 3. When he can't hear any traffic. 4. She finds it noisy and crowded. 5. Unemployment; they look for work in the towns. 6. The pub and a monthly disco. 7. There are so few of them that they feel conspicuous and as though they are being watched. 8. They get a driving-licence or buy a moped as soon as they are old enough. 9. They get married and have children there, then flee back to the country for peace and relaxation.

4 Buying and Selling

Shopping

Shopping is a popular topic for role-play and for listening comprehension, i.e. Speaking and Listening skills. You therefore need to be very familiar with a variety of fairly simple strategies, to be able to ask questions and answer them in all kinds of buying and selling situations.

Shopping Requirements

You have to cope with every aspect of being in a shop, from the greeting, through a catalogue of what you want to buy, including sizes, colours, amounts, etc., to the final reckoning, payment, words of thanks and farewell.

Location

You must be able to say where individual shops are to be found and how to get there.

Types of Shop and Products

Department store (and all the different departments), supermarket, street market, greengrocer, baker, etc. Popular shopping items are gifts, souvenirs, postcards, food and clothes, but do not forget less obvious possibilities such as the chemist or the shoe shop.

Payment

How much does it cost? How much does it come to? You must understand and respond to prices in German, Austrian or Swiss currency, both spoken and on price tickets. Is it expensive? Where do you pay?

Returns and Complaints

If goods are faulty or unsatisfactory in other ways – for example, wrong size or type – you should be able to explain the problem and ask for an exchange or a refund.

Useful Expressions

Whatever you are buying or selling, there are certain standard expressions in German which are used over and over again. These are listed below. Do remember, however, that the English phrases are only equivalents of the German expressions – they are not literal translations. Compare, for example, the literal translation of the German expression *Haben Sie sonst noch einen Wunsch?* with its equivalent English phrase.

Beim Kaufen (Buying)

Wo kann ich ... kaufen?	Where can I buy ... ?
Haben Sie ... Do you have ... ?	
Ich möchte ... / Ich hätte gern ...	I would like ...
Ich suche ...	I'm looking for ...
Kann ich ... anprobieren?	Can I try on ... ?
Kann ich ... umtauschen?	Can I exchange ... ?
Was macht das?	How much does it come to?
Was kostet ... ?	What does it cost?
Das ist mir zu teuer	That's too expensive
Haben Sie etwas Billigeres?	Have you something cheaper?
Ich nehme den/die/das/die	I'll take it/them
Das ist alles / Das wäre es	That's all

Beim Verkaufen (Selling)

Was darf es sein? / Womit kann ich Ihnen dienen?	Can I help you?
Was wünschen Sie, bitte?	What would you like?
Haben Sie sonst noch einen Wunsch? / Darf es noch etwas sein? / Außerdem noch etwas?	Will there be anything else?
Welche Farbe möchten Sie?	Which colour would you like?
Welche Größe tragen Sie?	Which size do you take?
Das macht DM 9,80	That comes to DM 9,80
Zahlen Sie bitte an der Kasse	Please pay at the till

- Make sure you know all these questions and expressions and are able to use them yourself, especially in oral work.

Further Food for Thought

- Description of a shopping trip.
- Special offers.
- Opening and closing times.
- Deliveries.
- Discussion of shopping habits and preferences.

- Comparison of items and prices.
- Comparison of difference between *Apotheke* and *Drogerie*; advantages and disadvantages of *Tante-Emma-Laden* and *Supermarkt*.
- Trying on clothes.
- Shop announcements and notices and signs.
- Labels and instructions on goods.

Speaking Practice

If you do not have a suitable partner, try expressing both sides of the following conversations in German. The answers to these Speaking exercises are on the tape.

Role-play 1
You are on an exchange visit to your German pen-friend. You want to buy your friend's mother some flowers as a birthday present, and you discuss this with your friend.
a) Ask what sort of flowers she likes.
   (Roses)
b) Ask if there is a florist's shop nearby.
   (Yes, round the corner between the supermarket and the bank)
c) Ask if the flowers are expensive in that shop.
   (Not really, and it is the only florist's in the town)

Role-play 2
You are in the florist's discussing your purchase with the shop assistant.
a) Say you are looking for a birthday present for your friend's mother and would like to give her some flowers.
   (What sort of flowers?)
b) Say she likes roses.
   (Yellow or white ones? or both? How many? They cost 80 pfennigs each)
c) Say you would like 7 white ones and 8 yellow ones.
   (O.K. That comes to 12 marks altogether)

Role-play 3
Build up a two-way conversation from the following situation, using the guide-lines and information provided.

You have bought a blue sweater and when trying it on at home you find a hole in the sleeve. You take it back to the shop. Ideally, you would like a replacement as the sweater is just what you are looking for.

a) Open the conversation by explaining the problem.
b) Respond to any questions put to you.
c) Decide what to do.
   Catch: They do not have another blue sweater in your size.

Writing Practice

Write a letter to your German pen-friend about your plans for Christmas, with the main emphasis on your Christmas shopping. Include the following points:
a) A suitable beginning to the letter.
b) Your plans to buy Christmas presents next weekend.
c) Say how many presents you must buy.
d) Give details about four presents, one for a friend, the other three for different named relatives.
e) Say you are hoping to buy most of them in a department store and ask your friend about his/her Christmas shopping.
f) A suitable ending with best wishes for Christmas and the New Year.

Here are two specimen answers, one at Basic Level, the other at Higher Level, to give you guidance on what is expected at each level and how the two levels differ in standard.

Basic Level Answer

Leicester, den 30. November

Lieber Helmut,

geht es Dir und Deiner Familie gut? Bald kommt Weihnachten und ich muß am Wochenende zehn Geschenke kaufen!

Ich gehe mit meiner Schwester Sylvia zum großen Kaufhaus. Sie bekommt ein Armband von mir. Für meine Mutter kaufe ich Ohrringe, für meinen Vater eine Sporttasche. Ich will für meinen Freund Paul eine Platte kaufen. Hoffentlich kann ich alles im Kaufhaus bekommen. Mußt Du auch viele Geschenke kaufen?

Ich wünsche Dir und Deiner Familie ein frohes Weihnachten und viel Glück im Neuen Jahr,

Dein Mark

Higher Level Answer

Leicester, den 30. November

Lieber Helmut,

hoffentlich geht es Dir und Deiner Familie gut. Uns geht es im Moment sehr gut. Welche Pläne hast Du für Weihnachten? Ich muß mindestens zehn Geschenke kaufen und ich gehe am Wochenende mit meiner Schwester Sylvia einkaufen. Wir hoffen, die meisten Sachen bei Scotts, dem großen Warenhaus, kaufen zu können. Sylvia kann ihr eigenes Geschenk aussuchen. Sie hat ein Armband gesehen, das ihr gefällt. Mutter bekommt Ohrringe, und für Vater kaufe ich eine neue Sporttasche. Für meinen Freund Paul hoffe ich auch etwas in der Sportabteilung zu finden, vielleicht eine Lampe für sein neues Rad.

Mußt Du auch so viele Geschenke kaufen? Was macht Ihr in Deutschland zu Weihnachten? Ich wünsche Dir und Deiner Familie ein schönes Weihnachtsfest und viel Glück im Neuen Jahr,

Dein Mark

Reading Practice

1. Read the following article about jeans.

Eine Arbeitshose wird gesellschaftsfähig

Jeans – die Hose der Goldsucher, Cowboys und Arbeiter. Aber nicht mehr lange. Die 50er Jahre bringen einiges in Bewegung. Auch in der Mode.

Einer muß beginnen. Wie so oft sind amerikanische Film- und Pop-Stars (Marilyn Monroe, Marlon Brando, Elvis Presley...) die Vorbilder für die Jugend in aller Welt. Sie machen Mode.

„„... denn sie wissen nicht, was sie tun", heißt ein amerikanischer Film. James Dean spielt einen Teenager – natürlich in Jeans – der von seinen Eltern nicht verstanden wird.

Doch die Jugendlichen wissen ganz genau, was sie tun. Sie wollen anders sein als ihre Eltern. Sie wollen sich distanzieren von der Welt der Erwachsenen. Die Kinder wollen ihr neues Selbstbewußtsein ausleben. Auch oder gerade in der Kleidung. Sie wollen nicht mehr lieb und nett sein, brav und schick aussehen wie die „Alten". Sie sind jung und wollen Jeans, hautenge Röhrenjeans. Nietenhosen, so heißen die Blue Jeans in Deutschland. Blue Jeans in allen Lebenslagen: in der Schule, in der Uni, beim Tanzen, auf Pop-Festivals, auf Pop-Konzerten, im Theater, in der Freizeit – überall Jeans. Die Jugendlichen kämpfen gegen ihre Eltern, Lehrer und andere Autoritäten. Jeans sind keine Kleidung mehr, sondern ein Symbol der Auflehnung. Jeans als Protest gegen einen gutbürgerlichen Lebensstil oder die bürgerliche Politik. Jeans, die Kleidung der Schüler und Studenten, der Kriegsgegner, Demonstranten, Gammler, Hippies, Beatniks, Alternativen . . . Jeans, die Uniform der Jugend.

Test Your Understanding

Answer these questions in English.
a) What point is the writer making in the second paragraph about American film stars and pop stars?
b) How would you translate the German title of the James Dean film mentioned here? (What is its English title?)
c) What problem, according to this article, does the teenager in the film have?
d) Give TWO reasons, expressed in the fourth paragraph, why young people want to wear jeans.
e) Give SIX situations mentioned here in which young people wear jeans.
f) List SIX groups of people whom the writer would expect to see wearing jeans.

Answers

a) They are models for young people all over the world. They make fashion. b) "They don't know what they are doing". (Rebel Without a Cause). c) His parents do not understand him. d) They want to be different from their parents. They want to disassociate themselves from the adult world. e) 6 of: at school, at university, when dancing, at pop festivals, at pop concerts, at the theatre, in their leisure time. f) 6 of: schoolchildren, students, pacifists, protesters, layabouts, hippies, beatniks, people with an alternative life-style.

2. Study the supermarket offers opposite.

Test Your Understanding

Answer these questions in English.
a) Give THREE facts about the cauliflowers.
b) Name THREE other vegetables mentioned here.
c) Give FOUR facts about the oranges.
d) Name FOUR other fruits which are on offer.

Reading Practice

e) What TWO claims are made for the kitchen towels?
f) There are two kinds of minced meat on offer. How are they different?
g) Name FOUR other products which are on offer.

Answers

a) 3 of: guaranteed fresh, French, large white heads, class 2. b) peas, beans, mushrooms. c) 4 of: guaranteed fresh, Italian, blood oranges, ideal for squeezing, class 2, in 2-kilo bags. d) grapefruit, lemons, pineapple, peaches. e) thick and absorbent (thirsty!). f) one is beef only, the other a mixture of beef and pork. g) whipping-cream, milk, German sausage, sugar.

Reading and Listening Practice
In the Department Store (Im Warenhaus)

Read the following dialogue which takes place in the Ladies' Wear department of a large store. The conversation can also be heard on the cassette. Helpful vocabulary is provided.

KARL-HEINZ: Guten Tag!
VERKÄUFERIN: Guten Tag! Kann ich Ihnen helfen?
KARL-HEINZ: Ich suche ein Geschenk für meine englische Freundin.
VERKÄUFERIN: Haben Sie etwas Besonderes im Sinn?
KARL-HEINZ: Einen Pullover vielleicht, einen roten. Ich habe schnell im Vorbeigehen einen im Schaufenster gesehen.
VERKÄUFERIN: Wissen Sie welche Größe sie trägt?
KARL-HEINZ: Na nu, das kann ich so ganz genau nicht sagen. Er darf nicht zu eng sein, wissen Sie, aber zu weit ist auch nichts. Könnten wir ihn umtauschen, wenn er nicht paßt?
VERKÄUFERIN: Kommt Ihre Freundin bald nach Deutschland? Wenn Sie ihre Größe nicht wissen, könnten Sie vielleicht zusammen den Pullover kaufen.
KARL-HEINZ: Ich wollte sie eigentlich damit überraschen.
VERKÄUFERIN: Das tun Sie bestimmt, wenn Sie ihr den Pullover aus dem Schaufenster schenken. Das ist nämlich ein Fußballhemd! Es gehört zu den anderen Sportartikeln im Fenster. Wenn Sie genauer hingeguckt hätten, hätten Sie den Spruch: ,,Fußballmeister – Neustadt'' darauf

	gesehen. Wir feiern damit den Sieg unserer Stadt in der Liga. Interessiert sich Ihre Freundin für Fußball?
KARL-HEINZ:	Das weiß ich auch nicht. Ich hab' sie im Sommer kennengelernt und Fußball ist eher eine Wintersportart, nicht? Vielleicht ist das mit dem Pullover keine so gute Idee. Ich schenke ihr ein paar Blümchen, wie die anderen es tun. Das ist aber so langweilig.
VERKÄUFERIN:	Warten Sie mal! Ich hab' einen Vorschlag. Wir haben ein Neustädter T-shirt in drei Größen: groß, mittelgross und klein. Bei T-shirts kommt es auf die Größe nicht so sehr an. Wie wäre es mit einem roten mittelgroßen Neustädter T-shirt?
KARL-HEINZ:	Das ist ja prima! Ich nehme es!

Vocabulary and Expressions

etwas Besonderes	anything in particular, something special	hingucken	to look
		der Spruch (¨-e)	slogan
		Fußballmeister (pl.)	football champions
im Sinn haben	to have in mind	feiern	to celebrate
im Vorbeigehen	while passing	der Sieg (-e)	victory, win
das Schaufenster (-)	shop window	die Liga (Ligen)	league
die Größe	size	sich interessieren für	to be interested in
eng	tight, narrow	eher	more, rather
weit	wide	der Vorschlag (¨-e)	suggestion
umtauschen	to exchange	auf etwas ankommen	to depend
passen	to fit	es kommt auf die Größe nicht so sehr an	size does not matter so much
überraschen	to surprise		
bestimmt	definitely		
gehören	to belong	das ist ja prima!	that's great!

Test Your Understanding

Answer these questions in English.
1. When and where has Karl-Heinz seen a red jumper?
2. Why does Karl-Heinz reject the assistant's suggestion that he and his girl-friend buy the jumper together?
3. What is special about the ''jumper'' Karl-Heinz has already seen?
4. Why is the shop making a special feature of it?
5. What idea does Karl-Heinz find boring?
6. What does he finally decide to buy?

Answers
1. In the shop window of the department store. 2. He wants it to be a surprise. 3. It is a football shirt. 4. It bears a slogan commemorating the victory of Neustadt in the football league. 5. Giving his girl-friend flowers. 6. A red, medium-sized Neustadt T-shirt.

Listening Practice
In the Department Store (Im Warenhaus)
Listen to the dialogue on the cassette which takes place in the Music department of the store. Useful vocabulary is given below.

Vocabulary and Expressions

die Platte (-n) record	**der Gutschein (-e)** gift token
der Zettel (-) piece of paper	**fallen lassen** to drop
herausholen to get out	**trotzdem** nevertheless
die Einkaufsliste (-n) shopping list	**schwärmen für** to be mad about, to be keen on
verwechseln to get mixed up	

Test Your Understanding
Answer these questions in English.
1. What is Christa trying to buy?
2. What are the items on the shopping list that she finds in her bag?
3. What suggestion does the shop assistant make?
4. Why does Christa decide in the end to follow this suggestion?

Answers
1. A record. 2. A cauliflower, 2 pounds of onions, 2 kilos of potatoes. 3. She should buy a gift token. 4. She thinks she might get the wrong record if she buys it herself as his taste in pop groups changes frequently.

5 Food and Drink

Eating Out

This includes eating and drinking in cafés, restaurants and other public places, and covers the whole process of getting food and drink – from walking through the door of a café feeling hungry and thirsty to paying the bill after a meal.

You need to be able to:
- find or ask for a table;
- summon the waiter/waitress;
- ask for a menu;
- discuss items on the menu;
- order food and drink for yourself and others;
- comment on the food;
- ask for and pay the bill and ask about service charges;
- ask for facilities available – for example, cloakrooms, toilets, telephone;
- make complaints or ask for extra crockery, cutlery, etc.

Eating at Home

This covers all the activities and customs concerned with preparing and eating food, including:
- meals – preparation, serving and clearing up;
- expressing hunger/thirst;
- likes and dislikes in food and drink;
- when and where meals take place;
- making requests for food or items on the table;
- refusing food or asking for more;
- expressions of enjoyment, appreciation, satisfaction;
- descriptions of food and drink.

39

Useful Expressions
Eating Out

Herr Ober! Waiter!
Fräulein! Waitress!
Die Speisekarte, bitte May I see the menu?
Was ist dieses Gericht, bitte? What is this dish?
Was kostet eine Portion . . . ? What does a portion of . . . cost?
Einmal Bratwurst mit Kartoffelsalat One sausage with potato salad

Zweimal Bratwurst mit Kartoffelsalat Sausage with potato salad twice
Möchten sie etwas dazu trinken? Would you like something to drink with it?
Ich möchte zahlen I would like to pay
Die Rechnung, bitte Bring me the bill, please
Das stimmt so Keep the change

Eating at Home

Guten Appetit!/Mahlzeit! Enjoy your meal!
Prost! Zum Wohl! Cheers! Good health!
Reichen Sie mir bitte . . . Please pass . . .
Wollen Sie mir bitte . . . reichen? Will you please pass . . . ?

Ich bin satt I am full, have had enough to eat
Hat's geschmeckt? Did you enjoy it?
Den Tisch decken/abräumen To set/clear the table
Lassen Sie es sich schmecken! Tuck in!

Speaking Practice

The answers to these Speaking exercises are on the tape.

Role-play 1

You are in a restaurant with a friend, ordering a meal from the waiter.
a) Can I have the menu, please?
    (Here it is)
b) One soup and one tomato juice, please.
    (Yes, sir/madam)
c) Then one roast beef with cabbage and potatoes, and one chicken and chips with peas.
    (Anything else?)
d) No, thank you, that's all.

Role-play 2

You are having a meal at your pen-friend's home and have forgotten to mention that you do not eat pork. Your friend's mother tells you the meal is roast pork. Develop the conversation, making these points:

a) Give a reason for not eating pork, apart from the fact that you simply do not like it, and apologise for not mentioning this sooner.
b) Discuss possible alternatives.
c) Decide on a solution.

Writing Practice

1. A friend is going to Germany on business and asks you to compile brief notes on getting a meal in a restaurant. Make notes in German, showing your friend how to express the following:
a) Summoning a waiter and asking for the menu.
b) Saying he/she would like a glass of white wine.
c) Saying he/she would like soup, pork with rice and salad.
d) Saying he/she would like stewed fruit for pudding.
e) Asking for the bill.

Answers
a) Herr Ober! b) Die Speisekarte, bitte. c) Ich möchte ein Glas Weißwein, bitte. d) Ich möchte Suppe, Schweinefleisch mit Reis und Salat. e) Ich möchte Kompott zum Nachtisch. f) Die Rechnung, bitte.

Specimen Question (NEA 1985)
2. Imagine that you are any one of the characters portrayed in the story below. Tell the story, in the past, using about 100 words in GERMAN.

Reading Practice

Specimen Answer

Here is one possible answer, suggested by the author.
Ich bin Wolf. Ich saß eines Tages in dem Café zur Linde, als ich meine alte Freundin Gisela sah. Sie hatte Joachim getroffen. Sie kamen zusammen ins Café und setzten sich an meinen Tisch. Joachim bestellte einen Eisbecher für Gisela und mich und eine Tasse Kaffee für sich. Ich hatte Gisela lange nicht gesehen, und wir hatten einander viel zu sagen. Joachim langweilte sich, denn wir hatten vergessen, daß er da war. Schließlich beschlossen Gisela und ich, ins Kino zu gehen, weil wir beide den neuen Film sehen wollten. Wir verließen das Café Hand in Hand, noch einmal gute Freunde. Der arme Joachim mußte die Rechnung bezahlen! (107 words)

Reading Practice

1. Study this restaurant menu, which is for a special birthday party.

hausgemachte Rinderkraftbrühe mit Grießklößchen
•
knackfrischer Salat
frisch vom Markt in Kräutersahnedressing
•
Stuttgarter Filetplatte
Schwein-, Rind- und Kalbsfilet zartrosa
gebraten mit einer Rahmsoße
von frischen Steinchampignons überzogen
Gemüsemosaik
Spätzle vom Brett, Kartoffelkroketten
•
Birne "Helene"
Vanille Eis mit Birnenhälfte belegt
und Schokoladensoße überzogen, Sahne
•
Kaffee
große Kuchenauswahl

Test Your Understanding

Answer these questions in English.
a) What is the main ingredient of the soup?
b) Where were the salad vegetables bought?
c) Name TWO meats offered as part of the main course.
d) The dessert is Pear "Helene". What are the FOUR ingredients?
e) What follows the dessert?

Answers

a) Beef. b) From the market. c) 2 of: pork, beef, veal. d) Vanilla ice-cream, pears, chocolate sauce, cream. e) Coffee with a selection of cakes.

Reading Practice

2. Read the following short article about drinks.

Limo billiger als Bier

In Gaststätten sind alkoholische Getränke meist billiger als Limo oder Cola. Ein Problem für Jugendliche. Ein Türke und ein Portugiese – sie haben eine Gaststätte in Troisdorf – wollen das „Kneipenproblem" lösen. Sie verkaufen alkoholfreie Getränke billiger als Bier. Jugendliche, Autofahrer und Anti-Alkoholiker können sogar kostenlos Mineralwasser trinken. Wer bezahlen möchte, spendet in eine Sammelbüchse für eine Hilfsorganisation.

Test Your Understanding
Answer these questions in English.
a) What problem is under discussion here?
b) Name THREE groups of people who can get free mineral water in this particular pub in Troisdorf.
c) What option is available to those who wish to pay for their mineral water?

Answers
a) In pubs, soft drinks tend to be more expensive than alcoholic ones. b) Young people, drivers and teetotallers. c) They can put money in a charity collecting-box.

3. The Kunert family have taken Karen to a local restaurant for Sunday lunch. You can read their conversation below. Helpful vocabulary is provided.

HERR KUNERT: Herr Ober, die Speisekarte, bitte!
OBER: Die Speisekarte, mein Herr.
GEORG: Ich weiß schon, was ich esse.
FRAU KUNERT: Ja Georg, du willst immer das gleiche essen, Bratwurst mit Kartoffelsalat. Willst du nicht zur Abwechslung etwas anderes probieren? Hähnchen mit Reis, zum Beispiel. Du mußt nicht unbedingt etwas Raffiniertes wählen, bloß weil wir nicht zu Hause essen, aber Bratwurst! Das kannst du doch an jeder Wurstbude kaufen!
GEORG: Vati hat gesagt, wir können bestellen, was wir wollen, und ich möchte Bratwurst!
HERR KUNERT: Laß ihn doch, Bärbel! Der Junge weiß jedenfalls, was er essen will. Ich habe noch keine Ahnung und möchte die Speisekarte in Ruhe studieren.

Reading Practice

KAREN: *(Pause, während alle die Speisekarte studieren)* Darf ich mal fragen, was Eisbein ist? Das klingt wie etwas Kaltes.
FRAU KUNERT: Nein, Kind, das ist ein typisch deutsches Gericht, Eisbein mit Sauerkraut und Erbsenpüree. Das ist Schweinefleisch auf eine besondere Art zubereitet, und ich möchte vorschlagen, daß du ein bißchen länger wartest, bevor du es probierst. Du solltest vielleicht Hähnchen bestellen, oder den Rinderbraten, bis du dich an die deutsche Küche richtig gewöhnt hast.
KAREN: Was essen Sie, Frau Kunert?
FRAU KUNERT: Wahrscheinlich den Kasseler Rippsbraten. Das ist ein Braten von geräuchertem Schweinefleisch mit einer dunklen Soße, und ich finde ihn sehr schmackhaft. Wenn du gern Geräuchertes ißt, dürfte es dir auch schmecken. Probier es mal, wenn du Lust hast.
OBER: Möchten Sie bestellen?
HERR KUNERT: Na, meine Damen, was habt ihr gewählt? Ich nehme das Eisbein, bitte, und einmal Bratwurst mit Kartoffelsalat für den Jungen da. Und du, Karl-Heinz?
KARL-HEINZ: Ich nehme auch das Eisbein, bitte, Vater.
FRAU KUNERT: Karen und ich möchten das Kasseler, bitte, Dieter.
HERR KUNERT: Also, nochmal Eisbein und zweimal Kasseler Rippenbraten, bitte.
OBER: Möchten Sie etwas trinken?
HERR KUNERT: Ja, bitte. Ein Pils für meinen älteren Sohn, eine Cola für den jüngeren. Eigentlich sollte man Bier zu dem Eisbein trinken, aber heute geselle ich mich zu den Damen und wir trinken eine Flasche Weißwein. Haben Sie einen Oppenheimer Krötenbrunnen?
OBER: Den haben wir bestimmt, mein Herr.

Vocabulary and Expressions

zur Abwechslung for a change
probieren to try, to sample
nicht unbedingt not necessarily
etwas Raffiniertes something exotic
wählen to choose
bloß simply, only
die Wurstbude (-n) hot-dog stand

keine Ahnung no idea
klingen to sound
sich gewöhnen an to get used to
der Braten (-) roast meat
geräuchert smoked
die Soße (-n) sauce, gravy
schmackhaft tasty
sich gesellen zu to join

Test Your Understanding

Answer these questions in English.
a) What does Georg want to eat?
b) How does his mother react to his choice?
c) What sort of dish is *Eisbein*?
d) What does Frau Kunert recommend to Karen to begin with, and why?
e) Describe the dish which Frau Kunert chooses for herself.
f) What drinks does Herr Kunert order, and for whom?

Answers

a) Fried sausage with potato salad. b) She does not understand why he always orders the same very ordinary dish. c) It is a typical German dish, knuckle of pork served with pickled cabbage and puréed peas. d) She recommends chicken or roast beef because Karen has not yet got used to traditional German dishes. e) It is a roast of smoked pork with a dark gravy. f) He orders lager for Karl-Heinz, cola for Georg and white wine for his wife, Karen and himself.

Listening Practice

In the Kitchen (In der Küche)

Listen to the first dialogue on the cassette between a German mother, Frau Thomas, and her son Gerhard's English pen-friend Michael, who is staying with them. Useful vocabulary is given overleaf.

Listening Practice

Vocabulary and Expressions

die Frikadelle (-n) rissole, meatball
die Salzkartoffeln boiled potatoes
der Blumenkohl cauliflower
gehacktes Fleisch minced meat
mischen to mix
feingehackte Zwiebel finely chopped onion
geriebenes Brot breadcrumbs
braten to fry
gar cooked through, done
klingen to sound
schälen to peel
der Nachtisch (-e) pudding
zeigen to show
genau exactly
die Quarkspeise a cold pudding made with curd cheese, sugar and fruit
rühren to stir, to beat
der Quark curd cheese
der Zitronensaft lemon juice
die Rosine (-n) raisin

Test Your Understanding

Answer these questions in English.
1. Where is Gerhard?
2. What are the Thomases having for lunch?
3. Name the ingredients for the meat dish.
4. Why does Michael decide to peel the potatoes?
5. What other contribution does he make towards preparing the meal?
6. Which two fruits are needed for the pudding?

Answers

1. Having a guitar lesson. 2. Meatballs with boiled potatoes and cauliflower. 3. Minced meat, finely chopped onion, breadcrumbs and egg. 4. The meatballs sound too complicated for him. 5. He makes the pudding. 6. Lemon and raisins.

Listening Practice

Before Lunch (Vor dem Mittagessen)

Now listen to the second dialogue between Frau Thomas and Michael, which takes place a little later. Useful vocabulary is given below.

Vocabulary and Expressions

das Tischtuch (¨-er) table-cloth	**der Streifen (-)** stripe
die Schrankwand (¨-e) wall unit	**riechen** to smell
die Schublade (-n) drawer	**sich einen Appetit holen** to work up an appetite
das Besteck cutlery	
das Messer (-) knife	**sowieso** in any case
die Gabel (-n) fork	**große Augen machen** to be surprised/wide-eyed
der Löffel (-) spoon	
servieren to serve	

Test Your Understanding

Answer these questions in English.
1. Where can Michael find the tablecloth?
2. What does Frau Thomas tell him not to forget?
3. Describe the dinner plates.
4. Where are the plates to be found?
5. Why will Herr Thomas and Gerhard arrive home together?
6. What will surprise Gerhard about the meal, according to his mother?

Answers

1. In the wall unit in the bottom drawer on the left. 2. The large serving spoons. 3. Large with a blue stripe. 4. In the kitchen cupboard next to the window. 5. Herr Thomas is picking Gerhard up from his guitar lesson. 6. The fact that Michael made the pudding.

6 School and Work

In School and After School

This is a very popular choice of topic in examination questions, especially for writing, as examiners like to choose subjects which they know candidates are familiar with and should be able to write about. Work is a less direct topic and may involve career plans, parents' occupations, and Saturday and holiday jobs, for example.

School

You should be able to talk and write about all of the following:
- Type of school.
- Daily school routine.
- Timetable.
- Homework.
- Timing of school day – that is, when school begins and ends, how many lessons there are, and how long they last.
- Breaks and lunch hour.
- Timing of holidays and events on school calendar.
- Subjects, subject choices and favourite subject(s).
- Examinations, tests and reports.
- Uniform.
- Extra-curricular activities, including clubs, sport, music and school trips.
- School buildings and class-rooms.
- School rules and punishments.
- School dinner arrangements.
- Future school plans – for example, A-Level choices.

Work

You should also be able to talk and write about:
- Your own future plans for further study and/or work.
- The occupation or profession of other people, including their attitudes, likes and dislikes.
- Working abroad.
- Work routine and earnings.
- Location of work and travel to and from work.
- Problems of unemployment and illness.
- Holiday and Saturday jobs, and applications for these.

Reading Practice

1. Read the following article about a student job.

GUTEN ABEND, DORT ENTLANG

Carsten, 19 Jahre alt und Schüler in Mainz, hat einen Job als Kontrolleur im Kino. Einmal in der Woche arbeitet er elf Stunden am Stück, ab 12 Uhr mittags. Bei langen Filmnächten kann es auch mal 5 Uhr morgens werden. ,,Eintrittskarten kontrollieren ist nicht anstrengend und außerdem kann ich in den Pausen sogar noch für das Abitur lernen", meint Carsten, ,,aber die Atmosphäre ist anonym. Wenn ich ,guten Abend' sage, kommt von den Leuten meistens keine Reaktion. Da könnte genausogut ein Automat stehen." Aber die Bezahlung (400 Mark im Monat) stimmt. Das Geld braucht Carsten, der noch bei seinen Eltern wohnt, für sein Auto.

Fast in allen Mainzer Kinos darf Carsten kostenlos die neuesten Filme anschauen. ,,Mein absoluter Kultfilm ist Monty Pythons ,Das Leben des Brian', den habe ich mindestens dreizehnmal gesehen." Beruflich hat er mit dem Kino nichts im Sinn. Er will Mathematik und Physik studieren.

Test Your Understanding

Answer these questions in English.
a) Where does Carsten work?
b) How many hours does he usually work at a stretch?
c) What is his work?
d) What complaint does Carsten have about the cinemagoers?
e) What is Carsten saving up for?
f) What perk goes with the job?
g) How often has Carsten seen ''The Life of Brian''?
h) What are his plans for the future?

Answers

a) At a cinema. b) 11 hours. c) He checks the tickets. d) He gets no reaction from them when he says: ''Good evening''. He might just as well be a machine. e) A car. f) He can see the latest films for nothing in nearly all the cinemas in Mainz. g) At least 13 times. h) He wants to study maths and physics.

2. Read the following article about work experience.
N.B. This is a difficult exercise!

Berufe testen? Wo kann man das? – Beim Betriebspraktikum! Drei Wochen lang können die 15- bis 16jährigen Schüler der Mittelstufe in einer Firma das Arbeitsleben kennenlernen.

„Toll, drei Wochen keine Schule!" Peter freut sich schon auf paradiesische Zeiten. Das wird sich erst zeigen, denke ich für mich. Ich bin der Klassenlehrer dieser 9 R 2, die in den nächsten Wochen ihr Betriebspraktikum machen soll. Alle Schüler der vorletzten Klassen (die 8. Klasse in der Hauptschule und die 9. in der Realschule) haben diese Möglichkeit. Sie sollen Erfahrungen in der Arbeitswelt sammeln: Berufe und Produktionsabläufe kennenlernen und den Umgang mit Menschen in der Arbeitswelt.

Einige Wochen lang haben wir uns vorbereitet. Wir haben Lebensläufe und Bewerbungen geschrieben und die Jugend-Arbeits-Gesetze durchgenommen. (Verboten sind zum Beispiel Akkord-Arbeit und körperliche Strafen.) Wir haben über Versicherungen gesprochen und mit einem Computer nach den besonderen Neigungen und Fähigkeiten jedes Schülers gesucht.

Einige Schüler fanden dann selbst eine Stelle für ihr Praktikum, andere bekamen Hilfe von der Schulleitung.

An diesem Freitag freuen sich alle. Es ist der letzte Schultag vor dem Praktikum. Jeder hat eine Stelle gefunden. Auf meinem Tisch liegt die Liste von Firmen: eine Autowerkstatt, ein Hotel, ein Reisebüro, eine Bank, eine Bäckerei, eine Versicherung, eine Krankenkasse, die Stadtverwaltung, ein Supermarkt, ein Fotolabor, ein Postamt, ein Krankenhaus, ein Zahnarzt . . . Es ist fast alles dabei. Aufgeregt stellen die Schüler noch letzte Fragen (natürlich sind alle schon besprochen):

„Wie lange müssen wir höchstens arbeiten?" (sechs Stunden täglich) „Wieviel Mittagspause steht uns zu?" (30 Minuten) „Müssen wir jeden Tag hin?" (sonntags nicht, und ein Werktag ist frei) „Bekommen wir Geld dafür?" (Nein. Aber ihr sollt auch nicht als billige Arbeitskraft eingesetzt werden, sondern lernen und probieren!) „Was ist bei Krankheit?" (Schule anrufen und den Betrieb)

„Tschüß, . . . und viel Spaß!" wünsche ich allen. Denn am Montag geht's los.

Test Your Understanding

Answer these questions in English.
a) How long does the work experience last?
b) Who is the writer of the article?
c) What can the pupils learn from work experience, according to this article?
d) How have the young people prepared themselves for their work experience?

e) What did they use a computer for?
f) Name TWO ways in which placements were found.
g) Give TEN examples of organisations which have offered work-experience placements.
h) What is the maximum number of hours which the young person can work each day?
i) How many days off do young people have per week?
j) What must they do if they are ill?

Answers

a) 3 weeks. b) The form teacher. c) They can get to know about professions and production processes, and learn how to get on in the world of work. d) They have written a curriculum vitae and letters of application; they have studied the laws concerning young people working. e) They used it to work out the inclinations and abilities of the students. f) Some found their own; others were helped by the school. g) 10 of: car repair workshop, hotel, travel agent, bank, baker's, insurance company, health insurance organisation, local government office, supermarket, photographic laboratory, post office, hospital, dentist. h) 6 hours. i) 2 days. j) Telephone school and work-place.

Reading and Speaking Practice

Read the passage below, describing the part-time job of Vera, a student.

DARF'S ETWAS MEHR SEIN?

Dreimal in der Woche muß Vera (24) um fünf Uhr morgens aufstehen, denn dreimal in der Woche ist Markttag in Mainz. Bis um vier Uhr nachmittags ist Vera dann auf den Beinen und verkauft griechische und italienische Spezialitäten. Vor allem Oliven. Zwanzig Sorten schwarze und grüne Ölfrüchte verbreiten ihren delikaten Duft. „Um die Mittagszeit geht's rund. Da komme ich mit dem Bedienen kaum nach. Aber sonst ist auch mal Zeit für ein Schwätzchen mit den Kunden."

Vera studiert Innenarchitektur und muß selber ihr Geld verdienen. Sie hat ihre Eltern früh verloren und bekommt auch keine staatliche Förderung. So arbeitet sie manchmal auch noch am Abend im Theater in der Künstlergarderobe. Während der Vorstellung muß sie den Schauspielern beim An- und Ausziehen der Kostüme helfen.
Zwei Jobs an einem Tag. Kann man da auch noch studieren? – „Ich liege vielleicht ein Semester zurück. Aber das muß ich in Kauf nehmen. Anders geht's eben nicht."

Here is one side of an interview with Vera. Her answers are supplied and you have to provide the questions, using the information in the passage you have just read as a guide. The answers are given on the tape.
FRAGE:
ANTWORT: Ich arbeite auf dem Markt.

FRAGE:
ANTWORT: Dreimal in der Woche.
FRAGE:
ANTWORT: Ja, ich muß um 5 Uhr aufstehen.
FRAGE:
ANTWORT: Um 4 Uhr nachmittags.
FRAGE:
ANTWORT: Griechische und italienische Spezialitäten, vor allem Oliven.
FRAGE:
ANTWORT: Um die Mittagszeit.
FRAGE:
ANTWORT: Innenarchitektur.
FRAGE:
ANTWORT: Ich habe auch einen Job abends im Theater.

Writing Practice

Here is an examination question taken from the NEA Summer 1988 paper.

You receive the following letter from your German penfriend:

> Lieber Darren / Liebe Lesley!
>
> Vielen Dank für Deinen letzten Brief. Hast Du Lust, mir in Deinem nächsten Brief etwas über Deine Schule zu schreiben? Ich möchte gerne wissen, wie es in der Schule in England ist. Mir geht es gut - wie geht es Dir und Deiner Familie? Hoffentlich auch gut!
>
> Tschüß!
>
> Dein Christian / Deine Christine

Write a letter in reply in GERMAN.
In the letter you should include the following:

- a suitable beginning and ending;
- when your school begins and ends;
- when the dinner hour is;
- TWO things you do in the dinner hour;
- details about your homework and how long you spend on it;
- the lesson you like best and why you like it;
- TWO other things about your school.

Write about 60 words. There is no need to count the number of words.

Reading and Writing Practice

a) Louise writes a letter to Dagmar, telling her about the English school system and her own typical school day. Read Louise's letter carefully and make sure you understand it before going on to the second part of this question. Helpful vocabulary is provided on page 54.

Moortown, den 3. November

Liebe Dagmar!

Servus! Und paß' auf! Du hast mich nach der Schule gefragt und jetzt kannst Du über einen typischen Schultag im Leben von Louise Mortimer lesen.
Ich muß um 7³⁰ aufstehen, denn der Schulbus fährt um 8¹⁵. Wir müssen um 8⁴⁵ im Klassenzimmer sein, wo unser Klassenlehrer, Mr. Hanson, feststellt, ob alle Schüler da sind. Wenn wir zu oft zu spät kommen, kriegen wir es im Zeugnis eingetragen!
In einer englischen Schule beginnen wir den Tag mit einem kurzen einfachen Gottesdienst. Die erste Stunde beginnt um 9¹⁵. Die Stunden dauern je 35 Minuten und sind meistens Doppelstunden. Es sind 8 Stunden am Tag, d.h. 40 in der Woche, Montag bis Freitag. Wir haben zwei Pausen von je einer Viertelstunde und eine große Mittagspause. Die dauert von 11⁵⁰ bis 1⁰⁰.
Die meisten Schüler essen in der Schulkantine. Es gibt Selbstbedienung, und das Essen ist gar nicht schlecht. Ich esse fast jeden Tag Salat und Joghurt, weil ich die schlanke Linie behalten will!
Im Sommer mache ich wichtige Prüfungen. Wir nennen sie „GCSE". Ich habe 8 Fächer, Englisch (Sprache und Literatur), Mathe, französisch, Deutsch (natürlich!), Geschichte, Physik und Chemie. Ich habe

auch andere Fächer im Stundenplan, Religion, Sport und Musik. Für mich sind das Entspannungs= stunden, denn wir müssen für die Prüfungsfächer ganz schön pauken.
  Nächstes Jahr beschränke ich mich auf drei Hauptfächer für meine A Levels. Das ist wie Euer Abitur. Ich werde mich auf Physik, Chemie und Mathe spezialisieren, da ich später Medizin studieren will.
  Im Moment trage ich noch Uniform in der Schule, einen dunkelgrünen Rock, eine dunkelgrüne Jacke und eine weiße Bluse, aber im nächsten Schuljahr brauche ich sie nicht mehr anzuziehen. Ihr dürft tragen, was Ihr wollt, nicht wahr? Vielleicht kannst Du mir eine Kassette schicken, auf der Du Deine Schule beschreibst, und inwiefern Euer Schulsystem anders ist als das bei uns. Dann kann ich die Kassette in der Deutschstunde spielen, und die ganze Klasse kann hören, wie es in einer deutschen Schule zugeht.
  Also sage ich für heute Tschüß!
          Deine Louise

Vocabulary and Expressions

das Zeugnis (-se) school report	pauken to swot, to work hard
der Gottesdienst (-e) act of worship, prayers	sich beschränken auf (+ Acc.) to limit oneself to
die Selbstbedienung self-service	das Hauptfach (¨-er) main subject
die Prüfung (-en) examination	das Abitur German school-leaving examination (equivalent of A Levels)
das Fach (¨-er) subject	
eine Entspannungsstunde (-n) lesson where you can relax	inwiefern how, to what extent

b) Write an account in German for a German school magazine, of your school in England, using Louise's letter as a guide. Pay particular attention to describing aspects of your school life which you think will be different from the German school system. To achieve Higher Level standard, you must write in greater detail than demanded in the Writing Practice question on pages 52 and 53, and must express some worthwhile opinions. Try to write a good account without using those hackneyed old favourites *interessant* and *langweilig*!

Listening and Speaking Practice

Interview with a Pupil (Interview mit einer Schülerin)

In return for Louise's letter, Dagmar sends her a cassette on which Karen interviews her about the German school system and her typical school day. Listen to their conversation, using the vocabulary below to help you.

Vocabulary and Expressions

die Fremdsprache (-n) foreign language	**die Mitteilung (-en)** message
sich vorbereiten to prepare oneself	**der Erfolg (-e)** success
	toi, toi, toi! good luck! touch wood!
die Ganztagsschule full school day (as in the English system)	

When you have heard and understood the interview, rewind to the beginning and play it again, this time stopping the tape after each question and giving your own answer, using the information given in Louise's letter on pages 53 and 54 for guidance.

7 Sport and Leisure

Free Time and Entertainment

This unit covers all kinds of activities, depending largely on personal taste and choice. It includes hobbies, pastimes, interests, games, amusements, competitions, clubs and societies. There are indoor and outdoor activities; activities for the individual and group activities; activities which you watch and activities in which you participate.

All of these can be considered under two headings: Sport and Outdoor Pursuits, and Entertainment and Interests.

Sport and Outdoor Pursuits

You should be able to:
- Name and express an opinion on the main kinds of sport – for example, football, tennis, athletics, hockey, swimming.
- Discuss in greater detail any sport in which you participate or have a particular interest.
- Say where your local sports centre, swimming-bath, football stadium, etc. is and say something about it, such as hours of opening, size, nature and quality of facilities offered, entrance fee.
- Buy a ticket for a sporting event and say where you would like to sit, if relevant.
- Discuss other outdoor interests and pursuits, such as camping, walking, winter sports, water sports, climbing, fishing, cycling, gardening.

Entertainment and Interests

You should be able to:
- Name and express an opinion on different kinds of entertainment, such as theatre, cinema, television, radio, music, festivals, circus.
- Discuss your own hobbies and interests, clubs and societies, and ask others about theirs. These may include: collecting stamps, postcards, etc., youth clubs, sports clubs, drama, photography, painting, reading, pets, pop music, discos, classical music, learning a musical instrument, quizzes, competitions, needlework, knitting, computers, card and board games. These are just a few of the many possibilities.
- Describe a visit to a zoo, safari park, museum, stately home, castle, amusement park, etc.

Reading Practice

1. Read the following article about trial-biking.

Trial: nicht nur Tempo – nicht nur Technik – nicht nur für harte Männer

Der Motor jault und knattert. Blauer Qualm schießt aus dem Auspuff. Es stinkt nach Benzin. Michael setzt den Sturzhelm auf und blickt prüfend ins Gelände. Der zwölfjährige Junge will mir zeigen, wie man mit dem Motorrad „den Hang" hinauffährt. Ich stehe unten und schaue hinauf. Für mich sieht dieser Hang eher wie eine Wand aus. Mindestens vier Meter geht es fast senkrecht in die Höhe.

Michael gibt Gas. Wie ein Jockey steht er auf den Stützen und rast auf den Hang zu. Noch zehn Meter. Dann reißt er den Lenker hoch. Jaulend schießt die schlanke Maschine den Berg hinauf. Die dicken Reifen schleudern schwarzen Dreck nach allen Seiten. Mit Mühe hält der Junge die Balance. Doch dann ist er oben. Michael strahlt. „Geschicklichkeit ist alles", sagt er nicht ohne Stolz. Das stimmt. Denn Tempo spielt beim Trial keine Rolle, Wichtig ist nur, mit möglichst wenig Strafpunkten durch die „Sektionen" – die verschiedenen Teile des Geländes – zu fahren. Strafpunkte erhält man zum Beispiel, wenn man den Fuß aufsetzt oder wenn man stürzt – was bei diesen schwierigen

Strecken öfters mal vorkommt. Auch wenn das Motorrad ein wenig rückwärts rollt, gibts einen Minuspunkt.

Das Trainingsgelände, auf dem Michael übt, war früher ein Schuttplatz und gehört heute einem Motorclub. Hier, am Rande eines Hamburger Industriegebietes, stört das Motorgeheul niemanden. Samstagnachmittag bei schönem Wetter ist hier was los: Der allgemeine Deutsche Automobil Club (ADAC) veranstaltet regelmäßig Trial-Übungskurse für junge Leute. Ein gutes Dutzend Jungen – und nur zwei Mädchen – im Alter von 7 bis 16 Jahren knattern mehr oder weniger geschickt mit ihren kleinen Motorrädern über das Gelände. Erst mit 16 Jahren bekommt man in der Bundesrepublik Deutschland eine Fahr-Erlaubnis für Motorräder. Aber auf Privatgelände braucht man keinen Führerschein. Und außerdem sind ja die Eltern dabei. Auf Campingstühlen sitzen sie am Rand, trinken Kaffee aus Thermos-Kannen und essen Kuchen. Aufmerksam verfolgen sie den Eifer ihrer Nachwuchs-Stars und freuen sich über ihre Leistungen.

Test Your Understanding

Answer these questions in English.
a) How does the motor-bike engine assault the ears, eyes and nose?
b) What precaution does Michael take before setting off?
c) How old is Michael?
d) What contrast is drawn between the machine and its tyres?
e) What, according to Michael, is the most important requirement for success?
f) Name THREE things for which you will get penalty points.
g) Give THREE facts about this training-ground.
h) About how many young people altogether use this training-ground for trial-biking?
i) Why are the under-sixteens able to use this training-ground, and by whom are they supervised?

Answers

a) It howls, roars, emits blue smoke and stinks of petrol. b) He puts on his crash-helmet. c) 12. d) The bike is slim but the tyres are thick. e) Skill. f) If you put your foot on the ground; if you fall off; if the bike rolls backwards. g) It used to be a waste tip; it now belongs to a car club; it is on the edge of an industrial part of Hamburg. h) 14. i) When driving on private land, it is not necessary to have a driving-licence; they are supervised by their parents.

2. Read the following account of life for two young musicians in a German youth orchestra.

Sehr in Eile kommt Nicola in die Cafeteria der Frankfurter „Alten Oper". „Es ist alles ein bißchen hektisch heute", entschuldigt sie sich. Nicola Borsche ist Mitglied der Jungen Deutschen Philharmonie. In wenigen Minuten beginnt die Probe vor dem Konzert am Abend. Und jetzt auch noch ein Interview! Die junge Geigerin weiß auch gar nicht, was sie sagen soll. Was soll sie erzählen von ihrem zukünftigen Beruf, der auch ihr Hobby ist und der ihr Leben ausfüllt? „Mein Vater ist auch Musiker – bei den Berliner Philharmonikern", sagt sie. „Ich bin mit Musik aufgewachsen, für mich gab es nie etwas anderes."
Nicola gehört dem Orchester seit zwei Jahren an und hat mit ihm auch eine große Tournee durch die USA gemacht. „Ich finde es einfach toll, daß man mit Musik alle Menschen erreichen kann – daß da nicht eine fremde Sprache dazwischen ist", schwärmt die 28jährige Berlinerin. Auch die riesigen Konzerthallen in den USA haben Nicola fasziniert. In Los Angeles spielte das Orchester mit rund 100 Musikern in einer Halle mit 17 000 Plätzen. „Der Saal war zwar nicht voll, aber es war dennoch überwältigend", erzählt Michael Graubner, der Pianist des Orchesters. Dem bärtigen Kölner gefiel besonders gut, daß die Amerikaner keinen Unterschied zwischen Pop, Jazz und Klassik machen. Er selbst macht nämlich auch sehr gerne Jazzmusik. Aber er hat auch die härtere Schule der Amerikaner erlebt: „Wir waren in einem musikalischen Workcamp. Da herrschte wirklich ‚Zucht und Ordnung'. Kein Nikotin, kein Alkohol, um zehn Uhr wird das Licht ausgemacht."

Test Your Understanding

Answer these questions in English.
a) In what ways is Nicola's violin-playing important to her?
b) What do you learn about her family?
c) How long has Nicola been a member of the orchestra?
d) What, for Nicola, is the special attraction of playing abroad?
e) Who is Michael Graubner?
f) Where does he come from?
g) What restrictions were imposed at the music work-camp in America?

Answers

a) It is her future profession and her hobby – her whole life, in fact. b) Her father is a musician with the Berlin Philharmonic. c) 2 years. d) That music has universal appeal – it breaks language barriers. e) The pianist in the orchestra. f) Cologne. g) No smoking, no drinking, lights out at ten.

3. Louise writes to Dagmar, telling her about how she spends her free time. Read Louise's letter on the next two pages. Helpful vocabulary is given on page 61.

Moortown, den 3. März

Liebe Dagmar!

    Vielen Dank für Deinen Brief und das Programmheft für das Schulkonzert. Du mußt schon sehr gut Geige spielen können, daß Du im Schulorchester Erste Geige spielst. Ich gratuliere Dir, und finde es toll, daß Ihr mit dem Konzert soviel Geld für die hungernden Menschen in der Dritten Welt aufgebracht habt. Wir haben auch solche Veranstaltungen in der Schule. Letztes Jahr haben wir über 1000 Pfund für soziale Zwecke eingenommen. Wir haben Autos gewaschen, Versteigerungen abgehalten und Briefmarken gesammelt.

    Als Beitrag zur Wohlfahrtskasse habe ich Hunde spazieren geführt, was mir auch viel Spaß gemacht hat, denn, wie Du schon weißt, habe ich Tiere sehr gern. Ich wollte sogar eine Zeitlang Tierärztin werden, aber das ist hier noch schwieriger als Ärztin zu werden. Man muß doch realistisch sein, wenn es um den Beruf geht. Katzen sind meine Lieblingstiere. Ich habe Dir schon Aufnahmen von meinen beiden Katzen, Flotsam und Jetsam, geschickt. Das heißt auf Deutsch Strandgut. Diese Namen haben wir ihnen gegeben, weil sie Findlinge sind!

    Du hast mich nach meinen Freizeitbeschäftigungen gefragt, und ich muß zugeben, daß ich im Moment nicht viel Zeit dafür habe. Tiere sind meine erste Liebe. Samstagmorgens helfe ich oft einem Tierarzt in seiner Sprechstunde. Ich sehe sehr gern Fernsehsendungen über Tiere und sorge natürlich für Flotsam und Jetsam.

    Ich höre gern Popmusik und habe Blockflöte gespielt, als ich viel jünger war. Ich treibe gern Sport, Turnen, Schwimmen, Hockey und Tennis. Am liebsten spiele ich Tennis. Ich hoffe bloß, daß meine Prüfungen vorbei sind, bevor das Wimbledon=

Reading Practice

> turnier beginnt. Nach den Prüfungen werde ich
> hoffentlich mehr Zeit für alles andere haben,
> obwohl ich auch einen Ferienjob haben möchte,
> um ein bißchen Geld zu verdienen.
> Was machst Du im Sommer? Vielleicht könnten wir
> uns treffen. Meine Eltern wollen im Juli nach Deutschland
> fahren, um meine Schwester Karen von den Kunerts
> abzuholen. Ich könnte mitfahren, wenn Deine
> Familie damit einverstanden ist. Dann kannst Du
> uns natürlich auch besuchen. Was hältst Du von
> meinem Vorschlag? Wenn Du dafür bist, können
> wir die Sache mit unseren Eltern besprechen.
>   Viele Grüße,
>   Deine Louise

Vocabulary and Expressions

Geige spielen to play the violin or fiddle	**das Strandgut** flotsam and jetsam
Erste Geige leader, first violin	**der Findling (-e)** stray (animal)
hungern to starve	**zugeben** to admit
aufbringen to raise (money)	**die Sprechstunde (-n)** surgery
die Veranstaltung (-en) event	**die Fernsehsendung (-en)** TV programme
soziale Zwecke charity	**sorgen für** to look after
die Versteigerung (-en) auction	**die Blockflöte** recorder
der Beitrag (¨e) contribution	**bloß** only
die Wohlfahrtskasse charity fund	**einverstanden mit** in agreement with
eine Zeitlang for some time	
wenn es um den Beruf geht where one's job is concerned	**der Vorschlag (¨e)** suggestion

Test Your Understanding

Answer these questions in English.
a) What do we find out about Dagmar's musical talents?
b) Why did Dagmar's school hold a concert?
c) Name THREE fund-raising activities mentioned by Louise.
d) What is Louise's own contribution to the charity fund-raising?
e) Why did Louise decide against studying veterinary sciences?
f) How did Louise's cats get their names?
g) Name THREE ways in which Louise demonstrates her love of animals.
h) What does Louise say about the Wimbledon tennis tournament?

Answers
a) She is the leader (i.e. first violin) in the school orchestra. b) To raise money for starving people in the Third World. c) Car-washing, auctions, stamp-collecting. d) Taking dogs for walks. e) It is more difficult than becoming a doctor. f) They were strays. g) She often helps a vet during surgery hours on Saturdays; she likes watching television programmes about animals; she looks after her cats. h) She hopes her examinations are over before it starts.

Listening Practice
A Big Day for Georg (Georgs große Chance)
Karl-Heinz's younger brother Georg has won a spot-the-ball competition. Part of the prize was free entry to a cup match. Later, Georg was interviewed for a feature on the local radio. Listen to the interview on the tape, using the vocabulary below to help you.

Vocabulary and Expressions

der Ehrengast (-̈e) guest of honour	die Präsidentenloge directors' box
das Preisausschreiben (-) competition	das Andenken (-) souvenir
ansehen to look at	sämtlich all
raten to guess	die Unterschrift (-en) signature
großartig great, splendid	versprechen to promise
der Eintritt (-e) entrance, entry	liefern to deliver
das Pokalspiel (-e) cup match	der Rechtsaußen outside right
dazu in addition	entscheidend decisive
einladen to invite	das Tor (-e) goal
	in deiner Ehre in your honour

Test Your Understanding
Answer these questions in English.
1. Who was the competition organised by?
2. How often does Georg go to watch football?
3. What did he do to win the first prize in the competition?
4. What else did the prize consist of, apart from free entry to the match?
5. What was Georg given as a souvenir of the day?
6. What other souvenir has he still to receive, and why must he wait for it?
7. What was the best moment of the day for Georg?
8. What does the interviewer offer to do in Georg's honour?

Answers
1. Geller, the big department store in Neustadt. 2. Every week. 3. He spotted the football in 5 out of 6 pictures. 4. An invitation to sit in the directors' box. 5. A

football signed by the team. 6. A souvenir T-shirt from Geller. He must wait because they have not yet been delivered. 7. When the outside right scored the decisive goal. 8. Play a record of his choice.

Speaking Practice

If you can find a partner for these two Speaking exercises, so much the better! The answers to Role-play 2 are on the tape.

Role-play 1

After listening to the radio interview with Georg, work out both sides of a similar interview on local radio about an important day in your life.

Role-play 2

You want to join a chess club and you have rung up Herr Giebel, the membership secretary. Work out the telephone conversation between you along the following lines:
a) Introduce yourself to Herr Giebel and say you want to join the chess club.
b) He asks you your full name (spell it out to him), address and age.
c) You provide this information and he asks you how long you have been playing chess and whether you play at school.
d) You tell him you have been playing for three years and belong to the school chess club. You play in the lunch hour.
e) Herr Giebel tells you the chess club meets once a fortnight on Fridays and is open from 6.00 p.m. until 10.00 p.m. He suggests you come to next week's meeting to see if you like it.
f) You tell him you will be there, say you are looking forward to it, thank him and end the conversation.

Writing Practice

1. Write up the interview suggested in Role-play 1 under Speaking Practice. This could be either a Basic or a Higher Level exercise, depending on how much detail is included. Remember that a Higher Level exercise must include some worthwhile expression of opinion.
2. Using Louise's letter to Dagmar on pages 60 and 61 as a guide, write a letter to your German pen-friend, discussing your free-time activities, sport, leisure, hobbies and interests. Choose your favourite pastime or interest and discuss it in detail. Conclude the letter by asking your pen-friend about his/her spare-time activities.

8 Holidays and Travel

Accommodation

One of the most important aspects of a holiday is accommodation, which can be considered under three headings:
1. Hotels and guest-houses;
2. Camping and caravanning;
3. Youth hostels.

Hotels and Guest-houses

You should be able, either in a letter or verbally, to ask for and book rooms, stating your requirements about type of room, length of stay, and facilities. You should be able to ask the following questions: Have you a room available? Double room? Single room? With bath? With shower? With WC? What does it cost per person per night? Are meals included? When do you serve breakfast? dinner?

You should also be able to:
- say whether you have booked;
- accept or reject a room;
- find out the room number and the whereabouts of the room;
- identify yourself;
- ask for your key;
- make complaints;
- ask where facilities are, such as TV room or post-box, in the hotel or nearby;
- ask for the bill.

Camping and Caravanning

You should be able to:
- book and ask for what you want as described in the previous section;
- say how many tents, caravans, vehicles or people the accommodation is for;

- ask about washing, shopping or eating facilities;
- ask about rules and regulations.

Youth Hostels

You need to know most of the above and should also be able to say you have a sleeping-bag or ask if you can hire one, and enquire about opening and closing times, meal times, dormitory arrangements and essential duties.

Further Food for Thought

- Discussion of holiday experiences and holiday plans, at home and abroad, including where, when, how long, with whom, the weather, hopes and expectations.
- Where relevant, be able to make particular reference to Germany and German-speaking countries and talk about group visits and exchanges.
- Use tourist information services – that is, ask for information, maps, brochures about a town and/or area; ask for details (location, cost, time) of excursions and places to visit; ask about accommodation. All this should be known for oral work and for letter-writing in particular, as well as for reading and listening comprehension.
- Supply information about travel documents, including passport; deal with customs checks; be able to change travellers' cheques and currency (see Unit 9: Services and Emergencies).

Travel and Transport

Travel is inevitably linked with holidays, but it also has other, more general applications, so it has its own independent section here.

You should be able to talk about transport generally, both public and private, say how you travel to school or work, understand and give information about other journeys.

Public Transport

You should be able to ask for, understand and give information about all forms of public transport, trains, buses, trams, aeroplanes, boats, e.g.:
- Arrival and departure times, use of timetables;
- Tickets, destination, single or return, class and day of travel and cost;
- The right platform or bus stand;
- The number of the bus and its route;
- Whereabouts of station, bus or tram stop, waiting-room, ticket office, information office, toilets, kiosks for refreshments or magazines/books;
- Necessity to change train or bus;
- Reserving a seat;
- Travelling by taxi.

Private Transport

You should be able to:
- buy fuel: petrol (also unleaded), diesel;
- ask someone to check oil, water and tyres;
- ask for and give information about routes, roads, traffic regulations, road conditions, diversions, parking;
- report a breakdown;
- discuss learning to drive;
- discuss hitch-hiking;
- describe a road accident.

Speaking Practice

The answers to this Speaking exercise are on the tape.

Role-play

You are at a railway station buying a return ticket to Düsseldorf.
a) I would like a second-class return ticket to Düsseldorf, please. How much is it?
 (That comes to 23,80 DM)
b) When is the next train?
 (The next train leaves at 10.33 from platform 4)
c) Can I get something to eat on the train?
 (Yes, this train has a dining-car)

Writing Practice

1. Your German pen-friend sends you a holiday postcard with the following message:

> Grüße aus Travemünde!
> Sehr heiß und sonnig, aber starkes
> Gewitter gestern. Wir bleiben morgens am
> Campingplatz, gehen nachmittags an den
> Strand. Wir haben zwei nette Jungen aus
> Köln kennengelernt. Wir gehen morgen
> mit ihnen segeln. Toll, nicht?
> Tschüß!
> Angelika

While you are on holiday in Austria you send her a postcard, giving her the following information:
a) The weather is quite warm and dry.
b) You get up early every day to swim in the lake.
c) You spend a lot of time with other young people.
d) Tomorrow you are having a trip to Vienna.

Answer
a) Das Wetter ist ganz warm und trocken. b) Ich stehe jeden Tag früh auf, um im See zu schwimmen. c) Ich verbringe viel Zeit mit anderen jungen Menschen. d) Morgen machen wir einen Ausflug nach Wien.

2. Write a formal letter to a German hotel on behalf of your parents, who are going on a business trip to Germany. You should:
a) Give the letter a suitable beginning and ending.
b) Say you are an English businessman travelling to Germany with your wife in the autumn.
c) Say you would like to spend three nights at the hotel, from 3rd October until 6th October.
d) Say you would like a double room with bath and WC, and would like half-board. Ask if it would be possible to have breakfast in your room.

e) Say you have a brochure from last year and would like to know if the charges are still the same.
f) Say you are travelling by car and would like to know about parking facilities.
g) Conclude by saying that you hope the hotel can offer you the accommodation you are looking for.

Answer

> Herrn J. Horn
> Hotel Lindenbaum
> Neustadt
>
> Exeter
> den 14. Mai
>
> Sehr geehrter Herr Horn,
> Ich bin ein englischer Geschäftsmann und ich fahre im Herbst mit meiner Frau nach Deutschland. Wir möchten drei Nächte in Ihrem Hotel wohnen, vom 3. bis zum 6. Oktober. Wir hätten gern ein Doppelzimmer mit Bad und WC und möchten Halbpension. Wenn möglich möchten wir in unserem Zimmer frühstücken.
>
> Ich habe eine Broschüre von Ihrem Hotel aus dem letzten Jahr und möchte wissen, ob die Kosten noch dieselben sind. Wir fahren mit dem Auto und möchten wissen, ob es bei Ihnen eine Parkmöglichkeit gibt.
>
> Ich hoffe, daß Sie uns die Unterkunft anbieten können, die wir suchen,
>
> mit freundlichen Grüßen,
>
> Edward Wilkins

Reading Practice

1. Here are two extracts from a Deutsche Bundesbahn brochure about holiday rail travel.

a) # Urlaubsreisen mit der Bahn

Diese Broschüre sagt Ihnen, warum es sich lohnt, mit der Bahn in den Urlaub zu fahren, und wie angenehm es ist, Urlaub von Anfang an zu machen.

Das zeigen nicht zuletzt auch die günstigen Angebote der Bahn, die Sie ebenfalls auf den folgenden Seiten kennenlernen werden. Und für jeden ist garantiert das Richtige dabei: für Einzelreisende genauso wie für Familien und Reisegruppen.

Für die Angebote, die mit einem * gekennzeichnet sind, gibt es noch ausführliche Prospekte von der Bahn. Und zwar überall dort, wo es Fahrkarten gibt.

Entdecken Sie die Vorteile des Urlaubs von Anfang an. Das ist oft billiger, als Sie vielleicht denken, und erspart Ihnen unterwegs unnötigen Streß und kilometerlange Staus. Kommen Sie gut in den Urlaub. Sicher, bequem und pünktlich mit der Bahn.

Reading Practice

Test Your Understanding
Answer these questions in English.
1. What are the TWO stated purposes of this brochure?
2. Name THREE kinds of rail traveller who might benefit from the information in the brochure.
3. What does an asterisk indicate?
4. Which THREE advantages does the brochure claim for rail travel?
5. A rail journey with the DB is summed up in three words in the brochure: ,,*Sicher, bequem und pünktlich*''. What do these three words mean?

Answers
1. To tell why it is worthwhile to use the train for holiday travel, and how pleasant it is to be on holiday from the start if you go by train. 2. People travelling singly, as a family, or in a group. 3. These are offers on which more detailed information is available. 4. It is often cheaper than you might think; it saves unnecessary stress while travelling; you don't get involved in long traffic hold-ups. 5. Safe, comfortable and punctual.

Fahr & Spar. Die neuen Preise der neuen Bahn.

Deutsche Bundesbahn DB

b)

TUI-FerienExpress

Mit dem TUI-FerienExpress fängt ihr Urlaub schon im Zug richtig an. Sie genießen den Komfort klimatisierter Abteile in verstellbaren Reisesesseln oder bequemen Liegebetten mit Klapptisch und Leselampe.

Und auch die Kleinen sind hier bestens aufgehoben: für sie gibt's einen erhöhten Fenstersitz.

Im TUI-Treffwagen können Sie unterwegs schon die ersten Urlaubsbekanntschaften schließen, wenn Sie an der Bar bei einem Bier vom Faß mit anderen Urlaubern ins Plaudern kommen. Während Sie Ihr Schwätzchen halten, vergeht die Zeit wie im Fluge – und es dauert nicht lange, bis Sie Ihr Urlaubsziel erreicht haben. Neben Reisen in die klassischen Feriengebiete Österreich, Jugoslawien, Spanien, Italien und Frankreich werden in bestimmten Verbindungen auch Autoreisezüge angeboten.

Ihr Wagenbetreuer serviert Ihnen unterwegs gerne kalte und warme Getränke im Abteil, während Sie schon so richtig in Urlaubsstimmung kommen.

Urlaub von Anfang an ist garantiert. Buchen können Sie bei allen DER-Reisebüros und den Fahrkartenausgaben der Bahn.

Reading Practice

Test Your Understanding
Answer these questions in English.
1. What is special about the seats in the TUI train?
2. Which extra facilities are available to passengers wanting to sleep on the train?
3. What special kind of accommodation is provided for small children?
4. Which drink is singled out for mention when referring to the bar facilities?
5. Name the FIVE countries regarded as classic holiday destinations.
6. Which additional rail service is offered on some routes?
7. What kind of refreshments may be offered to you in your compartment?
8. Where can you book for the TUI-FerienExpress?

Answers
1. They are adjustable. 2. There are comfortable sleeping berths, each equipped with pull-down table and reading lamp. 3. A raised window-seat. 4. Draught beer. 5. Austria, Yugoslavia, Spain, Italy, France. 6. Car transporters. 7. Cold and warm drinks. 8. In travel agencies and railway booking-offices.

2. Read the following letter which Mr. and Mrs. Mortimer have written to Herr and Frau Kunert about holiday arrangements. Helpful vocabulary is provided.

Moortown, den 3. März

Lieber Herr und liebe Frau Kunert,

Mit Hilfe unserer jüngeren Tochter Louise schreiben wir Ihnen diesen Brief. Erstmal möchten wir uns bei Ihnen sehr herzlich dafür bedanken, daß Sie unsere Tochter Karen in Ihre Familie aufgenommen und so gut für sie gesorgt haben. Wir wissen von ihren Briefen, daß es ihr bei Ihnen sehr gut gefällt und daß sie bei Ihnen sehr glücklich ist.
Sie wissen schon etwas über unsre Pläne für den Sommer. Wir wollen mit dem Wohnwagen nach Deutschland hinüberkommen. Das soll zum Teil unser Sommerurlaub sein, denn wir möchten gerne in den Schwarzwald fahren. Wir hoffen, dort Campingplätze zu finden. Dann können wir auf dem Weg nach Hause vorbeikommen und uns ein paar Tage auf dem Campingplatz in der Nähe von Neustadt aufhalten. Das wäre eine gute Gelegenheit, Sie kennenzulernen und zur gleichen Zeit unsre Tochter Louise zu der Familie ihrer Brieffreundin Dagmar zu bringen und Karen mit ihrem ganzen Kram nach Hause zurückzubringen. Dafür

> wird der Wohnwagen wohl sehr praktisch sein! Sie hat in ihren Briefen schon von dem großen Blumentopf geschwärmt, den sie von dem Warenhaus geschenkt bekommen hat, als sie damals die Ladendiebin erwischte.
> Wir wollen möglichst bald einen Termin abmachen und möchten vorschlagen, daß wir am 27. Juli bei Ihnen ankommen und bis zum 31. Juli bleiben. Schreiben Sie uns bitte, ob das bei Ihnen in Ordnung geht. Dann können wir alles andere danach erledigen.
>
> Herzlichste Grüße,
>
> Ihr Michael und Ihre Anthea Mortimer

Vocabulary and Expressions

sorgen für to look after	schwärmen to be keen or enthusiastic
vorbeikommen to call by	
sich aufhalten to stay	die Ladendiebin (-nen) (female) shop-lifter
die Gelegenheit (-en) opportunity	erwischen to catch
der Kram stuff, possessions, things	einen Termin abmachen to arrange a date
der Blumentopf (¨-e) plant pot	vorschlagen to suggest
	erledigen to settle, to sort out

Test Your Understanding

Answer these questions in English.
a) What do the Mortimers thank the Kunerts for?
b) Describe the Mortimers' holiday plans.
c) How do these arrangements involve the Mortimers' two daughters?
d) Why will the caravan prove to be particularly useful?
e) How did Karen acquire the plant pot mentioned by the Mortimers in the letter?

Answers

a) For accepting Karen into their family and looking after her so well. b) They want to take their caravan to Germany, to the Black Forest. On their way home, they will spend a few days at the caravan site near Neustadt. c) They will meet the Kunerts, drop their younger daughter Louise off to stay with Dagmar's family, and take Karen home with them. d) They can use it to accommodate all Karen's belongings. e) It was a present from the department store for catching the shop-lifter.

Listening Practice

The Dolls' Holiday (Der Puppenurlaub)

Karen, Karl-Heinz, Dorle and Norbert are strolling through Neustadt when they see a family preparing to go on holiday. Father is loading the car and, when everything is stowed away, a little girl appears from the house, pushing a doll's pram. Listen to the conversation on the cassette, using the vocabulary below to help you.

Vocabulary and Expressions

der Puppenwagen doll's pram	**das Eckchen** little corner, niche
leer empty	**höchstens** at best, at the most
sich freuen auf + Acc. to look forward to	**unterbringen** to accommodate
	einfach simple
der Kofferraum car boot	**anstrengend** tiring, strenuous

Test Your Understanding

Answer these questions in English.
1. What reason does Sabine give for wanting to take the doll's pram on holiday?
2. Where are the dolls?
3. Why does Sabine's father refuse to take the pram?
4. How did Sabine acquire the doll's pram?
5. What solution does the father suggest?
6. What comparison does he make between working and being on holiday?

Answers

1. Her dolls need their pram. 2. In her suitcase. 3. There is no more room in the boot. 4. It was a birthday present from her parents. 5. Putting it on the car roof. 6. He says working is much simpler – and much less strenuous!

9 Services and Emergencies

Agencies

There are many agencies which provide services, advice and practical help, including the post office, telephone, banks, tourist offices, lost-property offices, the fire brigade and the police. Other services you might need to use are dry-cleaners, hairdressers and repairs for watches, cameras, shoes, etc. (See also Unit 10: Health and Welfare, and Unit 8: Holidays and Travel).

- Remember: you should also be able to give information to a German person who does not speak English.

Post Office

You need to be able to:
- find out where a post office or letter-box is;
- find opening and closing times;
- buy stamps of particular denominations;
- ask how much it costs to send letters, postcards or parcels by inland post or abroad.

Telephone

You should be able to:
- find the whereabouts of a telephone or a call-box;
- follow instructions to make a call;
- ask for and give telephone numbers, including area codes;
- make a call and answer the telephone correctly;
- take a message and ask to speak to someone;
- get the operator and make a call abroad, reversing the charges if necessary;
- send a telegram.

Bank or Currency Exchange Office

You should have a good idea of what is involved in changing travellers' cheques or money. For example, you should:
- be able to say you would like to change travellers' cheques or money;
- be prepared to prove identity with your passport;
- be prepared to sign a form;
- be able to ask for coins or notes of a particular denomination.
  N.B. The banks and exchange offices often try to give you notes of a high denomination which may be awkward to change.

Writing Practice

Lost-Property Office
You must be able to:
- ask where to report a loss or find;
- say what the lost article is and describe it precisely, giving details of size, colour, shape, value, and any other relevant information;
- say when and where it was lost.

Writing Practice
Write a letter to your German pen-friend, telling him/her of an incident you witnessed. Here is the basic outline: You saw a car with the bonnet up and a man bending over the engine. Suddenly smoke started pouring from the engine, and then flames. The man stepped back, coughing, and fell down unconscious. You telephoned the fire brigade and the police, and called an ambulance. The services all responded promptly and you stayed until everything was under control. The police asked you to describe what you saw and you went to the police station to make a statement. Add further details to round out the letter.

Answer

Durham
den 22. September.

Liebe Angelika,

Wie geht's? Mir geht es gut und ich danke Dir für die Ansichtskarte aus Portugal. Ich muß Dir von einem Abenteuer erzählen, das ich erlebt habe.

Ich ging letzten Freitag zur Bushaltestelle, als ich einen Mann sah, der in den Motor seines Autos hineinschaute. Plötzlich kam Rauch aus dem Motor und dann sah ich Flammen. Der Mann trat hustend zurück und fiel bewußtlos zu Boden. Ich rief die Feuerwehr und die Polizei an und holte einen Krankenwagen. Sie kamen alle schnell, und ich blieb da, bis alles in Ordnung war.

Die Polizei hat mich gebeten, alles zu beschreiben, was ich gesehen hatte, und ich mußte auch zur Polizeiwache gehen, um eine Aussage zu machen. Der Autofahrer war, Gott sei Dank, nicht schwer verletzt. Er hatte Rauch eingeatmet, was sehr gefährlich sein kann. Das war ein aufregender Tag, nicht?

Schluß für heute: schreib bitte bald,

Deine Fiona.

Reading Practice

Karl-Heinz and Karen meet for coffee in the restaurant on the fourth floor of the department store where Karen works. Karen is already there when Karl-Heinz arrives. She is flushed and rather agitated. You can find out why by reading their conversation. Helpful vocabulary is provided on page 76.

KARL-HEINZ: Hast du schon bestellt?
KAREN: Ja, zwei Kännchen Kaffee, einen Bienenstich für dich und ein Stück Obsttorte für mich. Ist das in Ordnung?
KARL-HEINZ: Du bist ganz rot im Gesicht und scheinst etwas auf dem Herzen zu haben. Ist etwas los?
KAREN: Das kannst du wohl sagen! Ich bin eben von der Polizeiwache zurückgebracht worden. Ich war nämlich dabei, als eine Ladendiebin erwischt wurde, und als Augenzeuge mußte ich eine Aussage machen.
KARL-HEINZ: Was hast du eigentlich gesehen?
KAREN: Wie du schon weißt, wollte ich mir heute die Blumentöpfe ansehen. Meine Freundin in der Porzellanabteilung hat mir Bescheid gesagt, daß eine neue Lieferung aus Italien eingetroffen sei, und daß ich sie ja nicht versäumen dürfe. Du weißt ja, daß es in der Porzellanabteilung viele Spiegelwände gibt, damit die Glaswaren und das Porzellan im gespiegelten Licht so schön glänzen und glitzern. Ich guckte ganz zufällig in eine dieser Spiegelwände und hab' gesehen, wie dieses Mädchen eine kleine Porzellanfigur aufhob, als ob sie sie sich genauer angucken wollte. Dann hat sie die Figur einfach in die Tasche hineingesteckt. Sie ging dann ein

bißchen weiter zu einem Ständer mit Blumen aus Porzellan. Ohne den Rücken zu wenden, winkte ich meiner Freundin, die eben von der Kasse zurückkam. Ich zeigte ihr die junge Dame in der Spiegelwand, gerade als diese eine Porzellanblume in die Tasche fallen ließ. Hannelore holte schnell einen Ladendetektiv, der auch im Spiegel beobachtete, wie die Diebin noch etwas in die Tasche steckte. Er hat sie aufgefordert, ihm den Inhalt ihrer Taschen zu zeigen und man hat nach der Polizei geschickt. Da hab' ich sie natürlich zur Polizeiwache begleiten müssen, um eine Aussage zu machen.

Vocabulary and Expressions

der Bienenstich (-e) bee sting (here, a cake with a sugary top and cream or custard inside)
etwas auf dem Herzen haben to have something on your mind
das kannst du wohl sagen! you can say that again!
der Ladendieb (-e)/ die Ladendiebin (-nen) shoplifter
erwischen to catch
der Augenzeuge (-n, -n) eyewitness
die Aussage (-n) statement
sich ansehen to take a look at
die Porzellanabteilung (-en) china department
Bescheid sagen to tell, to inform

die Lieferung (-en) delivery
eintreffen to arrive
versäumen to miss
die Spiegelwand (¨e) mirror wall
spiegeln to reflect
glänzen to shine
glitzern to glitter
gucken to look
zufällig by chance
aufheben to pick up
der Ständer (-) stand
der Rücken (-) back
winken to wave, to gesticulate
fallen lassen to drop
beobachten to watch, to observe
auffordern to invite, to challenge
der Inhalt contents
begleiten to accompany

Test Your Understanding

Answer these questions in English.
1. What food and drink has Karen ordered?
2. Where has Karen come back from and what did she do there?
3. Why did Karen go to the china department today?
4. What is special about the walls in the china department?
5. What did Karen see a girl doing?
6. Where was Karen's shop assistant friend when Karen spotted the shoplifter?
7. What was the shoplifter stealing while Hannelore was watching her?
8. What did the store detective ask the girl to do?

Answers

1. Two pots of coffee, a bee-sting cake and a piece of fruit flan. 2. The police station, where she had to make a statement about helping to catch a shoplifter. 3. She wanted to look at the plant pots as a new delivery from Italy had just arrived. 4. Many of them are of mirror glass to make the glass and chinaware sparkle. 5. Picking up a small porcelain figure and putting it in her pocket. 6. Coming back from the cash desk. 7. A porcelain flower. 8. Show him the contents of her pockets.

Speaking Practice

The answers to these Speaking exercises are on the tape.

Role-play 1

Karen had the following conversation at the police station. Use the dialogue in the Reading Practice section to provide the questions which complete the interview.

FRAGE:
ANTWORT: Karen Mortimer.
FRAGE:
ANTWORT: Ich bin 18 Jahre alt.
FRAGE:
ANTWORT: Wiesenstraße 25.
FRAGE:
ANTWORT: Ich bin Studentin.
FRAGE:
ANTWORT: Ich arbeite bei Geller, in der Schreibwarenabteilung, aber ich wollte mir etwas in der Porzellanabteilung ansehen.
FRAGE:
ANTWORT: Es war Viertel nach zwei.

Role-play 2

You are in the lost-property office at the railway station because you left behind a small brown bag when you picked up your luggage. You hope that someone has handed it in.

a) (Can I help you?)
   I have lost a small bag.
b) (When and where did you lose it?)
   I left the station at half-past two with my luggage. I was standing at the barrier when I last had the bag. I forgot to pick it up with the rest of my luggage.

Listening Practice

c) (Can you describe the bag?)
It is quite small, about half a metre long, made of brown leather. It is quite old.
d) (What is inside it?)
I have made a list. It contains a Thermos flask, two paperback books, a newspaper, an apple, a bar of chocolate, some playing-cards, a blue pullover and a street plan of Cologne.
e) (Is this it?)
That looks like my bag. Can I have it, please?
f) (Please sign here and then you can have it)
Thank you very much. Goodbye!

Listening Practice

Listen to the next three dialogues on the cassette, which take place in different service agencies.

1. In the Post Office (Bei der Post)

Listen to the short conversation which Karen has in the post office. Useful vocabulary is given below.

Vocabulary and Expressions

die Waage	scales	**was macht das?**	how much does it come to?
insgesamt	altogether		

Test Your Understanding

Answer these questions in English.
a) What must Karen do with the packet she wants to post?
b) How much does she spend on stamps?

Answers

a) Put it on the scales. b) 4 marks.

2. In the Lost Property Office (Im Fundbüro)

Now listen to the dialogue which takes place in the lost-property office, using the vocabulary below to help you.

Vocabulary and Expressions

ausziehen	to take off (clothes)	**vorne**	at the front
die Bank (¨e)	bench, seat	**der Reißverschluß (¨e)**	zip
vorschlagen	to suggest	**abgeben**	to hand in
der Kragen (-)	collar	**unterschreiben**	to sign

78

Additional Listening Practice

Test Your Understanding
Answer these questions in English.
a) Why is Peter especially concerned about the loss of his anorak?
b) When was Peter in the park?
c) Why did he take off his anorak?
d) Where did he leave it?
e) Why did he leave that part of the park?
f) Whose idea was it to go to the lost-property office?
g) Describe the anorak.
h) Who found the anorak?
i) How long was the anorak at the lost-property office?
j) What did Peter have to do to get his anorak back?

Answers
a) It is fairly new. b) That morning. c) He was hot. d) On a bench. e) He wanted an ice-cream from a kiosk elsewhere in the park. f) It was the idea of Hans, his penfriend. g) Pale grey with a dark blue collar, a zip at the front and lots of pockets. h) A little girl. i) 10 minutes. j) Sign for it and pay one mark.

3. At the Dry-Cleaner's (In der Reinigung)
Listen to the conversation Frau Kunert has in the dry-cleaner's, using the vocabulary below to help you.

Vocabulary and Expressions

mit Appretur	with retexturing	**der Zettel**	ticket, slip
übermorgen	the day after tomorrow		

Test Your Understanding
Answer these questions in English.
a) What is Frau Kunert taking to be cleaned?
b) When will it be ready?
c) How much change will Frau Kunert get from a twenty-mark note?

Answers
a) A man's suit. b) The day after tomorrow. c) 7 marks, 20 pfennigs.

Additional Listening Practice
Lost and Found (Verloren und Gefunden)
Frau Kunert is preparing a meal in the kitchen when she realises that her wedding-ring is missing. Listen to the dialogue on the cassette, using the vocabulary below to help you.

Additional Listening Practice

Vocabulary and Expressions

einen Gefallen tun   to do a favour
der Ehering (-e)   wedding-ring
das Mehl   flour
nachschauen   to look, to check
sich vorstellen   to imagine
nirgends   nowhere
umsonst   in vain
der Spülbeckenabfluß   sink outlet
verschwinden   to disappear
schälen   to peel
der Abfalleimer (-)   waste bin
die Arbeitsfläche (-n)   work surface
der Herd (-e)   cooker
die Schürzentasche (-n)   apron pocket
der Kartoffelschäler (-)   potato peeler

verlorengehen   to get lost
spülen   to wash up
putzen   to clean
das Spülbecken   sink
der Klempner (-)   plumber
es bleibt mir nichts anderes übrig   I have no alternative
entdecken   to discover
der Abfluß   waste-pipe
abbauen   to dismantle, to take apart
trösten   to console
blitzsauber   as clean as a whistle
das Waschmittel (-)   cleaning agent
der Gummihandschuh (-e)   rubber glove
stark   strong

Test Your Understanding
Answer these questions in English.
1. What reason does Frau Kunert give Georg for not looking for the ring herself outside the kitchen?
2. Which rooms does she ask him to search in?
3. Why is she so surprised at losing the ring?
4. Where does Georg suggest looking?
5. Name FOUR other places where Frau Kunert has looked?
6. Where did Frau Kunert once find the potato peeler?
7. List THREE things which Frau Kunert did in the kitchen that morning.
8. What particular reason does Frau Kunert give for finding the ring as soon as possible?
9. What at first is the only consolation the plumber can offer to Frau Kunert?
10. Where precisely does the plumber find the ring?

Answers
1. Her hands are covered in flour. 2. Bathroom and bedroom. 3. She never takes it off. 4. The waste bin. 5. 4 of: kitchen table, floor, work surface, cooker, apron pocket. 6. In her apron pocket. 7. Washed up breakfast things, cleaned the floor and washed the lettuce. 8. She does not want her husband to find out. 9. That she will at least have a really clean sink outlet. 10. In a finger of the right-hand rubber glove.

Listening and Speaking Practice
After listening to the dialogue, work out the telephone conversation between Frau Kunert and the plumber, using the information given in the book and on the cassette.

Health and Welfare

How Do You Feel?

This topic is largely to do with how you are feeling and what to do when there is something wrong with you or some part of you. You should be able to:
- comment precisely on how you feel and ask how others feel;
- say where it hurts if you are in pain and ask for help or medical treatment;
- say you would like to rest or lie down or take pain-killers;
- make an appointment with a doctor or dentist;
- describe symptoms and discuss common ailments;
- buy medicines at the chemist's;
- describe a stay in hospital or a hospital visit;
- say whether you have health insurance.

Useful Expressions

Wie geht es dir? / **Wie geht es Ihnen?** How are you?	**Mir ist schlecht/übel** I feel sick
	Mir ist kalt/heiß I am cold/hot
Wie fühlst du dich? How do you feel?	**Mein Zahn tut mir weh** I have toothache
Was fehlt dir? What is the matter?	**Meine Füße tun mir weh** My feet are hurting
Was ist los? What is wrong?	
Es geht mir gut, danke Very well, thank you	**Ich habe Hunger** / **Ich bin hungrig** I am hungry
Es geht mir besser I am feeling better	**Ich habe Durst** / **Ich bin durstig** I am thirsty
Ich fühle mich krank/wohl I feel ill/well	**Ich habe Fieber** I have a temperature

Writing Practice

You are in Germany on an exchange visit. On returning home after a morning's outing, you and your friend find a note written by the mother. Reconstruct the note in German from the following information:

1. Stefan is ill; he has a temperature.
2. We are at the doctor's.
3. Your grandmother is still in bed because her leg hurts.
4. She must have her medicine at noon.
5. Are you two hungry?
6. You will find something to eat in the fridge.
7. We shall soon be back home.

Answers

Here are the equivalent German statements from which a note can be put together:

1. Stefan ist krank; er hat Fieber. 2. Wir sind beim Arzt. 3. Deine Oma ist noch im Bett, weil ihr Bein wehtut. 4. Sie muß um Mittag ihre Medizin haben. 5. Habt Ihr zwei Hunger? 6. Ihr werdet etwas zu essen im Kühlschrank finden. 7. Wir sind bald wieder zu Hause.

Speaking Practice

The answers to this Speaking exercise are on the tape.

Role-play

You are a teacher in the doctor's surgery.

a) (How can I help you?)
   Tell the doctor you have a very sore throat and can hardly speak.
b) (Have you any other symptoms?)
   Say you feel tired, but that is probably because you are coughing too much to sleep.
c) (I shall give you a prescription for cough medicine. It will also help you sleep)
   Ask how often you must take the medicine and ask how long it will take to get better as you are a teacher and cannot do your job without a voice.
d) (Three times a day. You should start feeling better after about five days)
   Say thank you and goodbye.

Reading Practice

Some people like to feel they can keep an eye on their welfare by looking at what astrologers have to say. Read the following:

Horoskop

Widder 21.3 bis 20.4
Der junge Frühling bringt allen Glück, die vor oder an dem ersten April geboren sind. Wenn Ihr Geburtstag auf ein späteres Datum fällt, erhalten Sie endlich die Nachricht, auf die Sie schon so lange warten.

Stier 21.4 bis 20.5
In den letzten Wochen haben Sie zuviel fürs Geschäft und zuwenig für sich getan. Wenn Sie sich schon keinen längeren Urlaub gönnen können, so genießen Sie wenigstens ein verlängertes Wochenende.

Zwillinge 21.5 bis 21.6
Wenn der Briefträger läutet oder das Telefon klingelt, sind es nur angenehme Nachrichten, die Sie erreichen. Beruflich sieht es ebenfalls rosig aus.

Krebs 22.6 bis 22.7
Lassen Sie sich von dem schönen Wetter nicht zum Faulenzen verführen. Nur mit Disziplin haben Sie die Chance, Ihr begehrtes Ziel zu erreichen.

Löwe 23.7 bis 23.8
Vorsicht bei einer neuen Bekanntschaft! Lassen Sie sich um Himmels willen nicht festnageln. Flirten ist jedoch erlaubt.

Jungfrau 24.8 bis 23.9.
Am Wochenende verleben Sie äußerst harmonische Stunden innerhalb der Familie und mit Freunden. Vergessen Sie nicht, wer Ihre wahren Freunde sind.

Waage 24.9 bis 23.10.
Das Leben zeigt sich wieder einmal von seiner schönsten Seite. Von Vorteil wäre es aber, sportliche Aktivitäten nicht zu übertreiben.

Skorpion 24.10 bis 22.11.
Gehen Sie geduldig mit älteren Menschen um, auch wenn es Ihnen schwerfällt. Besonders am Sonntag wird Ihnen ein Ausflug guttun.

Schütze 23.11 bis 21.12.
In den nächsten Tagen dürften sich Möglichkeiten bieten, die so schnell nicht wiederkommen. Halten Sie auch die finanziellen Vorteile vor Augen.

Steinbock 22.12 bis 20.1.
Es wird Zeit, ein paar Probleme in den Griff zu bekommen. Hilfreich wäre zu diesem Zweck, andere von Ihrem Standpunkt zu überzeugen.

Wassermann 21.1 bis 20.2.
Ihre persönlichen Finanzen sehen besser aus, als noch vor wenigen Tagen. Sie sollten aber mehr Rücksicht auf Ihre Gesundheit nehmen. Entspannen Sie sich am Wochenende bei einem guten Buch oder im Freundeskreis.

Fische 21.2 bis 20.3.
Sie wollen alles zur gleichen Zeit erreichen. Zum Erfolg gehören auch Umsicht und Planung. Neue geschäftliche Angebote sollten Sie erst einmal in Ruhe überdenken. So günstig, wie sie scheinen, sind sie leider nicht.

Test Your Understanding
Answer these questions in English.
1. At what time of the year did these horoscopes appear?
2. Into what two categories are Aries people divided for predictions in this horoscope?
3. What can Aries people in the second category look forward to?
4. What advice is given to Taureans?
5. Why do they need this advice?
6. What are the prospects for Gemini people?
7. What warning is given to Cancerians?
8. What should Leo people be cautious about?
9. What rather frivolous activity is permitted to Leos?
10. What kind of weekend can Virgo people anticipate?
11. What must Librans beware of overdoing?
12. With whom must Scorpios be patient?
13. Why is this an important time for Sagittarians?
14. What advice is given to Capricorn people about tackling their problems?
15. What are Aquarians urged to pay more attention to?
16. How should they spend the weekend?
17. What is the cautionary advice to Pisceans about business affairs?

Answers
1. Spring. 2. Those born before or on 1st April and those born after. 3. A long-awaited piece of news. 4. To take a break, a long weekend at the very least. 5. Recently they have been overworking and doing too little for themselves. 6. Good. 7. Not to be tempted to be lazy. They need discipline if they are to achieve their ambitions. 8. A new acquaintance. 9. Flirting. 10. A harmonious time with family and friends. 11. Sporting activities. 12. Older people. 13. Opportunities may arise which will not so soon be repeated. 14. They must try to convince others of their point of view. 15. Their health. 16. Relaxing with a good book or with friends. 17. They are to give some thought to any business offers as these may not be as favourable as they appear.

Listening Practice
Karen has Toothache (Karen hat Zahnweh)
Karen has toothache; after a couple of sleepless nights she plucks up the courage to tell Frau Kunert, who telephones the dentist for an appointment. Listen to the first dialogue on the cassette, using the vocabulary on page 87 to help you.

Listening Practice

Vocabulary and Expressions

der Termin (-e) appointment
nachschauen to check by looking something up
weh tun to hurt
eintragen to make a written entry (as in an appointment book)

Test Your Understanding

Answer these questions in English.
1. How long has Karen had toothache?
2. Why is Karen keen to go to the dentist as soon as possible?
3. What time is her appointment?

Answers

1. 2 or 3 days. 2. Her toothache is so bad. 3. 2.30 p.m.

Now listen to the second dialogue, which takes place at the dentist's. Useful vocabulary is given below.

Vocabulary and Expressions

das Sprechzimmer (-n) surgery
röntgen to X-ray
vorläufig for the time being
plombieren to fill (a tooth)
verschreiben to prescribe
die Entzündung (-en) inflammation, infection
die Behandlung (-en) treatment
kaum hardly, scarcely
höchstens at the most
erledigen to sort out, to settle

Test Your Understanding

Answer these questions in English.
1. Where is the dentist's waiting-room?
2. Where is the tooth which aches?
3. What made it hurt to begin with?
4. What does the dentist plan to do first?
5. Why does he prescribe tablets for Karen?
6. Why does he not prescribe penicillin?
7. How often may she take aspirins?
8. When should the treatment be completed?

Answers

1. On the right. 2. At the bottom on the left-hand side. 3. Hot drinks. 4. X-ray the tooth. 5. There is inflammation. 6. She is allergic to it. 7. 2 tablets every 4 hours at the most. 8. In 2 weeks time.

Grammar

This section contains a carefully chosen selection of those aspects of German grammar which students ask about most frequently and have the most difficulty in understanding. The points are illustrated with examples in German, for which a translation is provided where necessary or appropriate. The topics covered are:

Prepositions;
Personal Pronouns;
Adjective Endings;
The Comparative and Superlative Adjective;
Verb Tenses;
Modal Verbs;
Word Order.

Prepositions

Prepositions show us how nouns relate to each other. In German, all prepositions govern cases. This means that the noun affected by the preposition must be in the case governed by that preposition – e.g. in the sentence *Kurt geht aus dem Haus*, *aus* is the preposition and takes the dative case. Therefore, *Haus* must be in the dative, shown by *dem*.

Prepositions can be divided into four groups according to the cases they take. In the following lists, all the common prepositions are represented, but the lists are not complete. It can be misleading to give hard and fast English translations of prepositions, because they are so often used in idioms with different meanings, but the usual English equivalent is given with examples of the most important idiomatic uses.

Group 1: Prepositions Followed by the Accusative

The most common of these make up the useful mnemonic FUDGEBO:
für = for
um = round, at (with Time, *um neun Uhr*)
durch = through
gegen = against, about (with Time, *gegen halb vier*)
entlang = along (usually after the noun, *die Straße entlang*)
bis = as far as, until
ohne = without
e.g. *Dieter arbeitet für seinen Vater.*
   Dieter works for his father.

Wir gehen ohne dich, wenn du dich nicht ein bißen beeilst.
We shall go without you if you don't hurry up a bit.

Group 2: Prepositions Followed by the Genitive

There are very few common ones. These are the most useful:
trotz = in spite of
wegen = because of
während = during, in the course of
(an)statt = instead of

● The English 'of' is a useful reminder that these prepositions take the genitive.
  e.g. *Wir wollen trotz des schlechten Wetters einen Ausflug machen.*
  We want to have a trip out in spite of the bad weather.
  Wegen der Kälte trug sie zwei Pullover.
  Because of the cold, she was wearing two jumpers.

Group 3: Prepositions Followed by the Dative

aus = out of, from
mit = with (*mit dem Bus* = by bus)
bei = at the house of, with
nach = after, to (*nach Hause gehen* = to go home)
zu = to (*zu Hause* = at home, *zu Fuß* = on foot)
von = from, of
seit = since
außer = except (for)
entgegen = towards (usually follows noun)
gegenüber = opposite (usually follows noun)
e.g. *Boris Becker kommt aus Deutschland.*
  Boris Becker comes from Germany.
  Die Familie fährt morgen nach Frankreich.
  The family is going to France tomorrow.
  Anna geht noch zur Schule.
  Anna still goes to school.
  Ich lerne seit einem Jahr Deutsch.
  I have been learning German for a year.
  Er wartet dem Bahnhof gegenüber.
  He is waiting opposite the station.

Group 4: Prepositions Followed by the Accusative or Dative

The prepositions in this group need a more detailed explanation of the way they are used.

an = on, to, at, by
auf = on (horizontal surface like a table), to
hinter = behind
in = in, into
neben = beside, next to
über = over
unter = under, among
vor = in front of, before, outside
zwischen = between

With each of these prepositions, there is always the question: accusative or dative? Apart from a few idiomatic uses, the acid test is always this: are you expressing movement towards (accusative) or simply stating position (dative)?

Read the following story carefully and look at how these nine prepositions are used. Where motion towards is involved, you will see that the accusative follows the preposition; where position is being stated, without involving motion towards, the preposition is followed by the dative.

Mutter geht in die Stadt, um ihre Freundin zu besuchen. Ihre Freundin wohnt in der Stadtmitte neben einem schönen Park. Jeden Nachmittag geht die Freundin mit ihrem Hund in den Park, um ihn spazieren zu führen. Heute geht Mutter auch mit. Im Park sind viele Bäume und Blumen. Nach dem Spaziergang sitzen Mutter und ihre Freundin am Rand eines großen Rasenplatzes und beobachten die Kinder, die auf dem Rasenplatz Fußball spielen. Der Hund sitzt zwischen Mutter und ihrer Freundin und ist zuerst müde nach dem langen Spaziergang. Plötzlich sieht er aber den Ball und läuft auf das Gras, um ihn zu holen. Der Ball rollt hinter einen Baum und verschwindet. Er ist unter den gefallenen Blättern versteckt. Der Junge vor dem Baum ist der Torwart und er sucht den Ball. Er findet ihn unter den Blättern und wirft ihn über den Kopf des Hundes den anderen Kindern zu. Der Hund ist doch müde; seine Herrin nimmt ihn wieder an die Leine und sie gehen alle drei nach Hause.

Personal Pronouns

Pronouns are words which stand for nouns, i.e. for people or things, and there is much confusion in the use of pronouns. In a language like German, where every<u>thing</u> as well as every<u>body</u> has a gender, precision is very important. Using pronouns wrongly, especially in letters, can be a serious barrier to effective communication.

In English, everything is referred to as 'it', but in German every noun is either masculine (*der*), feminine (*die*) or neuter (*das*), and can therefore be *er*, *sie* or *es*. So, you need to know the gender of a noun in order to decide on its personal pronoun. Having established this point – for example, *der Tisch* must be *er*, *die Küche* must be *sie* and *das Zimmer* must be *es* – you then have to decide what part the pronoun is playing in its sentence. If it is the subject, it will be nominative; if it is the direct object, it will be accusative; and if it is the indirect object, it will be dative.

e.g.

Nominative *Der Stuhl steht in der Mitte.*
Er steht in der Mitte.

Accusative *Ich setze den Stuhl in die Ecke.*
Ich setze ihn in die Ecke.

Dative *Ich gebe dem Stuhl ein neues Bein.*
Ich gebe ihm ein neues Bein.

Here is a table of the German personal pronouns in the three cases illustrated above.

Nominative	*Accusative*	*Dative*	*English*
ich	mich	mir	I, me
du	dich	dir	you
er	ihn	ihm	he, him
sie	sie	ihr	she, her
es	es	ihm	it
wir	uns	uns	we, us
ihr	euch	euch	you
Sie	Sie	Ihnen	you
sie	sie	ihnen	they, them

Pay particular attention to the pronouns for 'you', in order to avoid confusion and misunderstandings. In modern English, we no longer use such forms as 'thou', 'thee' or 'ye'; 'you' covers everything. However, in German – and, indeed, in most other European languages – distinctions are still made when addressing others. You must decide whether you are speaking to one person or more than one, and (very important, this!) how well you know them. Once you have made your choice, stick to it. Germans will be understandably confused if you address them as intimates in one sentence and as a formal public meeting in the next! This is especially true if you do it in a letter.

There are two forms of address for 'you' in German: familiar and formal. How do you make the decision about which form to use?

The Familiar 'You'
Singular – *du*
Plural   – *ihr*

This form of address is used for people whom you know well, your family and friends and, up to the age of about twenty, for all the people you work or study with who are on the same level as you, or who are younger. Children up to the age of about sixteen are called *du* and *ihr* by everyone. Animals also fall into the *du* category.

The Formal 'You'
Singular ⎫
Plural   ⎬ *Sie* (N.B. capital S)

This is often known as the polite form and is used to address people in formal situations and people you hardly know.

Whenever you are dealing with people you do not know personally, it is best to address them as *Sie*. Later on, you may get to know them better, on a personal level, and then you can agree to change from *Sie* to *du*. In all formal situations, though, stick to *Sie* in the first instance. These situations include buying in shops, getting petrol, talking to receptionists, asking policemen for information or help, asking strangers for directions, talking to people at work who have authority over you or whom you do not know personally, talking to the parents of your pen-friend, and writing business letters.

Pronouns in Letter-writing
Another point to remember about letter-writing is that all the pronouns connected with *du* and *ihr* have capitals when used in letters.

e.g.

> Liebe Trudi !
>
> Danke für Deinen letzten Brief. Ich wünsche Dir Glück in Deinen Prüfungen. Wir freuen uns auf die Sommerferien, wo wir Euch alle in Bournemouth sehen werden, Dich und den kleinen Neville und die ganze Familie.

Adjective Endings

In German, the adjective has no ending when used after the verb *sein* (to be), e.g. *das Gras ist grün;* the grass is green. When the adjective is used with a noun, e.g. *das grüne Gras;* the green grass, it always has an ending.

If you find adjective endings difficult or confusing, it may be helpful to look upon the adjective as a lazy creature which will get away with doing as little work as possible. The function of an adjective ending is to give grammatical information about its noun, to tell you the number, gender and case of that noun. Where there is another word which supplies this information, the adjective need do no more than show a nondescript ending, such as *-e* or, especially, *-en*. It only has to work harder and show a meaningful ending, such as *-es*, *-em* or *-er*, where there is no other way of finding out the grammatical information.

 e.g. *Sie schreibt mit roter Tinte.*
  She writes with red ink.

The *-er* on *roter* tells you that *Tinte* is feminine, singular and dative. There is no other word which gives this grammatical information, so it must be shown in the adjective ending.

 e.g. *Die gelben Blumen sind für dich.*
  The yellow flowers are for you.

The definite article *die* shows that *Blumen* are nominative plural, so the adjective does not need to show this information and has the nondescript ending *-en*. This view of the adjective being lazy and only providing meaningful and informative endings when absolutely necessary can be seen to be foolproof when applied to the three tables of adjective endings which follow.

93

Adjective Endings

Group 1

These are the endings which the adjective takes when used after words which are declined like *der*. The most important of these are *der*, *dieser*, *jeder*, *welcher*. The endings on these words are strong, therefore the adjective used after them has weak endings, as you can see by looking at Table 1.

TABLE 1

	Singular			*Plural*
	masculine	feminine	neuter	
Nominative	der alte Mann	die alte Frau	das junge Kind	die jungen Menschen
Accusative	den alten Mann	die alte Frau	das junge Kind	die jungen Menschen
Genitive	des alten Mann(e)s	der alten Frau	des jungen Kind(e)s	der jungen Menschen
Dative	dem alten Mann	der alten Frau	dem jungen Kind	den jungen Menschen

Group 2

These are the endings which the adjective takes when used after words which are declined like *ein*. These are *ein*, *kein*, *mein*, *dein*, *sein*, *ihr*, *unser*, *euer*, *Ihr* and *ihr*. The endings on these words are partly strong and partly weak, so the adjective ending has to compensate where the ending is weak. You will see from Table 2 that the adjective has more work to do than after the Table 1 words. *Kein* is used to illustrate this set of endings, since *ein* has no plural form.

TABLE 2

	Singular			*Plural*
	masculine	feminine	neuter	
Nominative	kein alter Mann	keine alte Frau	kein junges Kind	keine jungen Menschen
Accusative	keinen alten Mann	keine alte Frau	kein junges Kind	keine jungen Menschen
Genitive	keines alten Mann(e)s	keiner alten Frau	keines jungen Kind(e)s	keiner jungen Menschen
Dative	keinem alten Mann	keiner alten Frau	keinem jungen Kind	keinen jungen Menschen

Group 3

These are the endings which the adjective takes when standing on its own, so they have to be strong endings. The only help the adjective has is in the masculine and neuter genitive singular, where the noun adds *(e)s* to show the case. Here you will see that the adjective reverts to its

preferred laziness and the ending is the weak -*en*. Otherwise, all the endings in this group are the strong endings you would expect to see.
N.B. -*en* can also be a strong ending providing grammatical information. It is the ending associated with the masculine accusative singular and the dative plural.

TABLE 3

	Singular			Plural
	masculine	feminine	neuter	
Nominative	schwarzer Kaffee	frische Milch	kaltes Bier	deutsche Weine
Accusative	schwarzen Kaffee	frische Milch	kaltes Bier	deutsche Weine
Genitive	schwarzen Kaffees	frischer Milch	kalten Biers	deutscher Weine
Dative	schwarzem Kaffee	frischer Milch	kaltem Bier	deutschen Weinen

The Comparative and Superlative Adjective

Forming the Comparative Adjective

In English there are two ways of forming the comparative adjective: by adding -er if the adjective is short, e.g. clean, cleaner, or by using more . . . with longer adjectives, e.g. interesting, more interesting. In German, however, there is only one way to form the comparative adjective and that is by adding -*er*, no matter how long the adjective is, e.g. *interessant*, *interessanter*. Most adjectives of one syllable with a, o or u in the word also add an umlaut, e.g. *lang, länger*.

If used in front of a noun, the usual adjective endings are added to the comparative adjective, e.g. *ein interessanteres Buch*, a more interesting book.

Forming the Superlative Adjective

The superlative is formed by adding -*st* or -*est* to the adjective, with an umlaut where appropriate. There is no other way of forming the superlative in German. The superlative is most often used with 'the', e.g. the biggest, the longest, so can best be expressed in German as:

der
die } *längste*   the longest
das

der   (*Film*
die } *interessanteste* { *Geschichte*   the most interesting { story
das   (*Buch*   { film
                                                     { book

Irregular Comparisons
There are some important irregular comparisons:
big:	groß	größer	der, die, das größte
good:	gut	besser	der, die, das beste
high:	hoch	höher	der, die, das höchste
near:	nah	näher	der, die, das nächste
much, many:	viel	mehr	der, die, das meiste

Verb Tenses

The Present Tense
There is only one present tense in German. This covers the three different ways we have in English of expressing the present:

e.g. *er macht* he makes; he is making; he does make

The form of the present tense of a German verb depends on whether it is weak or strong, e.g. *machen* is weak, *sehen* is strong:

```
         machen                              sehen
ich mache      wir machen          ich sehe       wir sehen
du machst      ihr macht           du siehst      ihr seht
Sie machen     Sie machen          Sie sehen      Sie sehen

er  ⎫                              er  ⎫
sie ⎬ macht    sie machen          sie ⎬ sieht    sie sehen
es  ⎭                              es  ⎭
```

Note the vowel change in the *du* and *er/sie/es* forms in the singular of *sehen*. This is quite a common feature in strong verbs, but does not happen with every strong verb. For example, *kommen* is like *machen* in the present tense. You just have to learn which strong verbs have a vowel change in the present tense.

The Future Tense
The future tense is not often used in German, since the present tends to be used instead where the context makes it clear that the future is intended. This makes the present an even more versatile tense, as the sentence *Ich spiele heute Fußball* can now be seen to have five possible meanings in English:
1. I shall play football today.
2. I play football today.
3. I am playing football today.
4. I am going to play football today.
5. I do play football today.

If the future tense is needed, it is formed with an auxiliary verb plus the infinitive, as in English. The auxiliary is *werden*. Here is the future tense of *spielen*:

ich werde spielen	wir werden spielen
du wirst spielen	ihr werdet spielen
Sie werden spielen	Sie werden spielen
er ⎫	
sie ⎬ wird spielen	sie werden spielen
es ⎭	

The Imperfect Tense

The imperfect tense is very versatile as well as being easy to use. It is the standard past tense used in all formal kinds of writing, such as books, newspapers and documents. In spoken German and more informal writing, especially letters, a mixture of the perfect and imperfect tenses may be used, more or less according to the user's personal choice. It is, however, common practice to use the imperfect tense for frequently used verbs such as *sein* and *haben*, and for the six modal verbs (*können, müssen, wollen, mögen, dürfen, sollen*) which are so often used with an infinitive depending on them. To show the versatility of this tense, here is a list of English translations of *ich ging*:

ich ging ⎰ I was going
⎨ I went
⎱ I used to go
    I did go

As usual with German verbs, the form of the imperfect tense depends on whether the verb is weak or strong. Here are examples of a typical regular weak verb and a strong verb in the imperfect tense: *machen* is weak, *sehen* is strong.

machen		*sehen*	
ich machte	wir machten	ich sah	wir sahen
du machtest	ihr machtet	du sahst	ihr saht
Sie machten	Sie machten	Sie sahen	Sie sahen
er ⎫		er ⎫	
sie ⎬ machte	sie machten	sie ⎬ sah	sie sahen
es ⎭		es ⎭	

The Perfect Tense

The perfect tense is frequently used in conversation and letters. The Germans often use this compound past tense, consisting of the auxiliary verb plus the past participle, where we would use the simple past in

Verb Tenses

English. For example, *Ich habe ihn letzten Samstag gesehen* translates best into English as: I saw him last Saturday. We would not say in English: I have seen him last Saturday. It is therefore not wise to equate the German perfect tense automatically with the English perfect tense. English is a much more complex language in its use of tenses.

As a compound tense, the perfect tense does require a lot of attention to detail. Here is advice on how to choose the correct auxiliary and how to form the past participle.

Haben or Sein?

Choice of auxiliary can be solved by asking yourself three questions about the verb you want to use:
1. Does the verb take a direct object?
2. Does the verb involve motion?
3. Does the verb show change of state?

Here are four examples which show how this approach works:
a) The bird has eaten the worm.
   1. Does the verb take a direct object?
   The answer is yes, so the auxiliary must be *haben: Der Vogel hat den Wurm gefressen*.
b) The children have gone into the café.
   1. Does the verb take a direct object?
   The answer is no, so the second question is asked:
   2. Does the verb involve motion?
   The answer is yes, so the auxiliary must be *sein: Die Kinder sind ins Café gegangen*.
c) Her uncle died on Saturday.
   1. Does the verb take a direct object? No.
   2. Does the verb involve motion? No.
   3. Does the verb show change of state? Yes.
   The auxiliary must be *sein: Ihr Onkel ist am Samstag gestorben*.
d) At that time he lived in this house.
   1. Does the verb take a direct object? No.
   2. Does the verb involve motion? No.
   3. Does the verb show change of state? No.

The auxiliary must be *haben* because all verbs for which the answer to question 2) or 3) is yes, have *sein* as the auxiliary: *Damals hat er in diesem Haus gewohnt*.

As so many verbs take a direct object, there is often no need to proceed beyond Question 1. Here are the rules on which the three questions are based:

Sein. Only verbs which express motion or change of state have *sein* as their auxiliary.
  e.g. *Mein Bruder ist gestern nach Deutschland gefahren.*
   My brother went to Germany yesterday.
   Der Hund ist hinter einem Baum verschwunden.
   The dog disappeared behind a tree.
  There are two exceptions to this rule – *sein* (to be) and *bleiben* (to stay, remain):
  e.g. *Es ist kalt gewesen.*
   It was cold, it has been cold.
   Wir sind zu Hause geblieben.
   We stayed at home.
  Haben. All verbs (except *sein* and *bleiben*) which do not satisfy the rules for *sein* have *haben* as the auxiliary. The largest group are those verbs which take a direct object:
  e.g. *Karen hat einen Blumentopf gekauft.*
   Karen has bought a plant pot.
  N.B. As reflexive verbs take a direct object in the form of the reflexive pronoun, they also fall into this category.
  e.g. *Johann hat sich schnell angezogen.*
   Johann quickly got dressed.

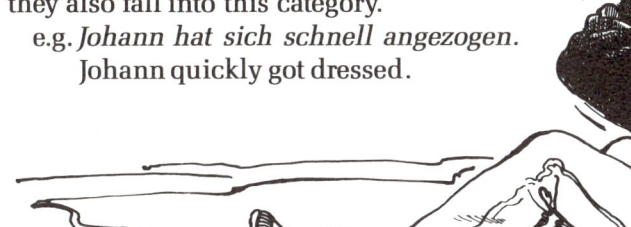

The Past Participle

Endings and beginnings. Past participles end in either *-t* or *-en*. All weak verbs have a past participle ending in *-t*, e.g. *gekocht* (*kochen*), *erreicht* (*erreichen*), *gewußt* (*wissen*). All strong verbs have a past participle ending in *-en*, e.g. *gebrochen* (*brechen*), *gegangen* (*gehen*), *verstanden* (*verstehen*). This is significant because you can always tell by looking at its past participle whether a verb is strong or weak. As strong verbs tend to have irregular forms, the *-en* on the past participle is a useful warning sign.

Most past participles begin with the prefix *ge-*, e.g. *gekocht* (*kochen*), *gegangen* (*gehen*), *gekauft* (*kaufen*), but there are exceptions:

Verb Tenses

1. Separable verbs. These verbs consist of a movable prefix plus main verb, e.g. *aufmachen, hereinkommen*. When used in the perfect tense, the past participle of the main verb is used, with the separable prefix at the front of it, e.g. *aufgemacht, hereingekommen*:
Ich habe die Tür aufgemacht.
I opened the door.

2. Inseparable verbs. The prefix on these verbs is immovable, so it is not possible to insert an extra *ge-*. Some of these verbs already begin with *ge-* in any case, e.g. *gehören* (to belong to), *gefallen* (to please). An inseparable verb therefore has no extra *ge-* in the past participle, but it does, of course, end in *-t* or *-en* depending on whether it is weak or strong, e.g. *erreicht* (*erreichen*), *verkauft* (*verkaufen*), *verstanden* (*verstehen*), *gehört* (*gehören*), *gefallen* (*gefallen*).

3. Verbs ending in *-ieren*. These are verbs of foreign origin which came into the German language relatively recently, mostly from French, e.g. *interessieren, studieren, telefonieren, gratulieren*. The past participle has no prefix, no *ge-*, but is otherwise treated as a weak verb and therefore ends in a *-t*, e.g. *interessiert, studiert, telefoniert, gratuliert:*
Karen hat sich sehr für Blumentöpfe interessiert.
Karen was very interested in plant pots.

Word order. The auxiliary verb is the main verb in the perfect tense and therefore obeys the rules governing a main verb in any sentence (see section on Word Order, page 104). The past participle belongs at the end of the sentence, but the auxiliary has priority as the main verb in a subordinate clause.
e.g. *Ich bin spät aufgestanden, weil der Wecker nicht geklingelt hat.*
I got up late because the alarm clock did not go off.

The Pluperfect Tense

This is the past tense which expresses what you had done or had been doing. The pluperfect takes you further back into the past than the perfect or imperfect tenses, and its form is a mixture of the two:
e.g. *Ich hatte ein Butterbrot gemacht.*
I had made a sandwich.
Ich war in die Stadt gegangen.
I had gone into town.

Modal Verbs

The six modal verbs are:
können, müssen, wollen, dürfen, mögen, sollen.

These crop up everywhere and it is not possible to hold a proper conversation in German without them. They often express attitude or intention and usually occur with another verb. We use their English equivalents constantly in much the same way, so the first step is to put the German and English together to show what the verbs actually mean. The two most useful bits are the *ich* and the *er/sie/es/man* forms, which happen to be identical in the six verbs, i.e. *ich kann, er kann*, so the *er* form is given below with its nearest English equivalent:

kann = can, is able to
muß = must, has to
will = wants (to)
darf = may, is allowed to
mag = likes (to)
soll = is to, is obliged to

e.g. *können:*
Ich kann die Schuhe nicht kaufen, weil ich nicht genug Geld habe.
I cannot buy the shoes because I do not have enough money.
müssen:
Er muß heute mit dem Bus fahren.
He must travel by bus today.
wollen:
Er will die Zeitung lesen.
He wants to read the newspaper.
dürfen:
Robert darf nur zweimal in der Woche Fußball spielen, weil er abends für die Schule lernen muß.
Robert is only allowed to play football twice a week because he has to do school-work in the evenings.
mögen:
Gisela mag nicht samstags einkaufen gehen.
Gisela does not like shopping on Saturdays.
sollen:
Der kleine Jürgen soll um 1900 Uhr ins Bett gehen, aber versucht immer länger aufzubleiben.
Little Jürgen is supposed to go to bed at seven, but always tries to stay up longer.

Modal Verbs

These are the most usual and straightforward meanings of these verbs. You can see from the examples that they are used as main verbs in a clause or sentence and are usually followed by another verb in the infinitive which goes at the end of that part of the sentence. This is a useful pattern, of which the most common variation is a question:
   e.g. *Darf Robert heute abend Fußball spielen?*
   May Robert play football this evening?
   Muß er heute mit dem Bus fahren?
   Does he have to go by bus today?

These verbs occur mostly in the present and imperfect tenses. Here are some of the same examples in the imperfect (or past) tense:
Ich konnte die Schuhe nicht kaufen, weil ich nicht genug Geld hatte.
I could not buy the shoes because I did not have enough money.
Er wollte die Zeitung lesen.
He wanted to read the newspaper.

Sometimes you will see *könnte*, *müßte*, *dürfte*, and especially and most importantly, *möchte*, i.e. a form which looks like the imperfect tense with an umlaut added. This is the imperfect subjunctive and gives the idea of 'might' or 'would' to the verb, e.g. *ich könnte* means I might or should be able to, *ich müßte* means I should or might have to, *ich dürfte* means I might be allowed to, and most useful of all, *ich möchte* means I should like (to).

You must be careful not to add the umlaut when all you want to do is to express an idea in the past tense:
   e.g. *Ich konnte ihr helfen.*
   I was able to help her.
As soon as the umlaut appears, you are changing the meaning:
   Ich könnte ihr helfen.
   I might be able to help her.

If you look again at the two German examples *Ich konnte ihr helfen* and *Ich könnte ihr helfen*, you will see that both could be correctly expressed by the English: 'I could help her', and this is one of the reasons for confusion and error with these verbs. English 'could' means both 'I was able to' and 'I might be able to'. Try not to be led astray in German by English ambiguities – and beware the umlaut!

N.B. No part of *wollen* or *sollen* ever has an umlaut!

Apart from *möchte* (would like), which is very useful and necessary in situations where wishes and requests are being expressed, it is best to avoid these forms of the past with an umlaut. Stick to saying what you <u>can</u> do and what you <u>were able</u> to do. However, it is worth repeating that

möchte is indispensable and it should be regarded as a useful formula for making wishes known:
e.g. *Sie möchte heute abend ins Kino gehen.*
She would like to go to the cinema tonight.
Möchtest du Edamer in deinem Käsebrot?
Would you like Edam cheese in your sandwich?

Another quirky aspect of these verbs concerns their frequent use with verbs of motion. The Germans so often use such expressions as:
Ich muß nach Hause gehen.
I must go home.
Wir müssen bald weggehen.
We must go soon.
that they tend to leave out the verb of motion completely and will say:
Ich muß nach Hause.
Wir müssen bald weg.

Word Order

Generally speaking, German word order is not so very different from English word order, but there are some important rules to be observed. Getting the word order wrong can be much more confusing and misleading than putting wrong endings on individual words. Take the following English sentence, for example:
I could not bake the cake because I could not find any eggs.
This makes perfect sense as it stands, but written down according to German word order rules, it would read:
I could the cake not bake because I no eggs find could.
This is nonsense!

Word Order

Similarly, if the German sentence:
Ich konnte den Kuchen nicht backen, weil ich die Eier nicht finden konnte.
was written down with English word order, it would be just as confusing as the English sentence in German word order.

N.B. The German examples in this section on word order are there to demonstrate German word order patterns and so they have been translated only where this was felt to serve a useful purpose.

Verbs in Main Clauses

All proper sentences have a main clause. In German, the main verb (that is, the finite verb) is the second idea:

e.g. *Ein alter Mann sitzt heute in dem roten Auto.*
Heute sitzt ein alter Mann in dem roten Auto.
In dem roten Auto sitzt heute ein alter Mann.

All three versions of this sentence are possible, but in each case the verb is the second idea. Sometimes, when two main clauses occur together, it can look as though the verb is not the second idea:

e.g. *Der alte Mann sitzt in dem roten Auto und wartet auf seinen Sohn.*

Und does not count in word order as it is a co-ordinating conjunction, so it may look as though *wartet* is the first word in the second clause. However, the pronoun *er* is understood before the verb *wartet*, so *wartet* is, in fact, the second idea:

Der alte Mann sitzt in dem roten Auto und (er) wartet auf seinen Sohn.

Verbs in Subordinate Clauses

In a subordinate clause, the main (or finite) verb belongs at the end of the clause:

      main clause   subordinate clause
Er hat jetzt keine Zeit, | *weil er den nächsten Bus erreichen muß.*

Notice the pattern of the verbs in a sentence which consists of a subordinate clause followed by the main clause:

e.g. *Weil er den nächsten Bus erreichen muß, hat er jetzt keine Zeit.*

The subordinate clause counts as the first idea in the whole sentence; it is separated by a comma from the main clause; and it has its own main verb at the end. This gives the typical pattern of verb, comma, verb.

Other Rules Concerning Verbs

The rules above concern main verbs. Other rules concern the position of infinitives and past participles, both of which belong, where possible, at the end of a clause or sentence:

e.g. *Sie wollen heute abend ins Theater gehen.*
Hast du meinen Fotoapparat gesehen?
In a subordinate clause, however, the main verb must go at the end, so the infinitive or past participle is placed just before the main verb, since the latter is more important:
e.g. *Ich bin sicher, daß er einen Monat in Spanien verbringen will.*
Wir glaubten, daß er mit seiner Frau auf Urlaub gegangen war.
Separable prefixes behave in much the same way. In a main clause, the separable prefix is placed at the end:
e.g. *Ich stehe jeden Morgen um sieben Uhr auf.*
In a subordinate clause, the prefix joins the verb at the end of the clause:
Wenn du nicht sofort aufstehst, bekommst du kein Frühstück!

Noun and Pronoun Objects

Where noun and pronoun objects occur together, there are rules about their position.
1. When two nouns occur together, one accusative and one dative, the dative noun comes first:
   e.g. *Ich schrieb meiner Mutter einen Brief.*
   I wrote my mother a letter.
2. When two pronouns occur together, one accusative and one dative, the accusative pronoun comes first:
   e.g. *Ich schrieb ihn ihr.*
   I wrote it to her.
3. When there is a noun and pronoun together, one accusative and one dative, the pronoun comes first irrespective of case:
   e.g. *Ich schrieb ihr einen Brief.*
   I wrote her a letter.
   Ich schrieb ihn meiner Mutter.
   I wrote it to my mother.

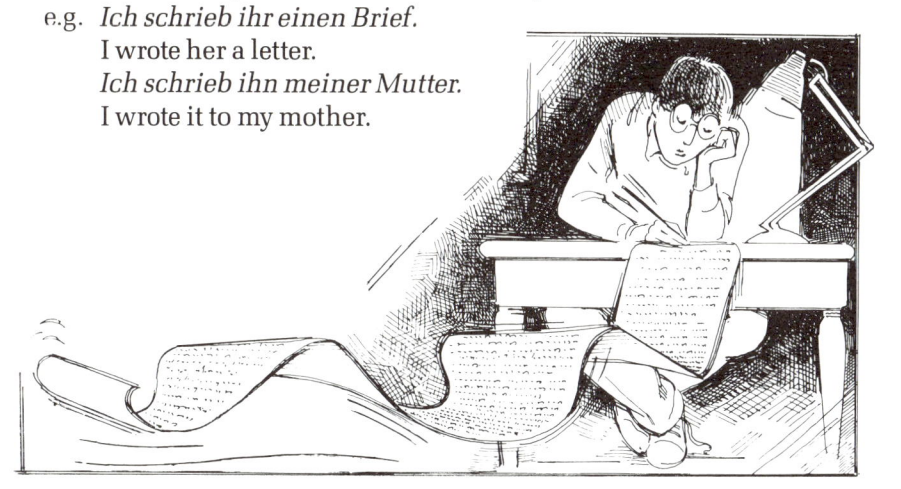

Word Order

Time, Manner, Place

Where two or three adverbs or adverbial phrases occur next to each other, they must be put in the order of Time, Manner, Place:

e.g. *Sie fahren jeden Tag mit dem Bus zur Schule.*
 They go to school every day on the bus.
 Er setzte sich ruhig in die Ecke hin.
 He sat down quietly in the corner.

The Position of *Nicht*

Usually, *nicht* goes at the end of a sentence or as near as possible to the end when there are other contenders for the final position:

e.g. *Wir haben ihn heute nicht gesehen.*
 We have not seen him today.

If, however, the *nicht* belongs with something in particular in a sentence, then it precedes this, so that the negative emphasis is in the right place:

e.g. *Sie wollten nicht zum Freibad gehen, weil es zu kalt war.*
 They did not want to go to the open-air swimming-pool because it was too cold.
 Wir saßen nicht im Parkett, weil uns das zu teuer war.
 We did not sit in the stalls because it was too expensive for us.

Speaking Test

Examination Technique and Useful Tips

This chapter contains helpful information on examination technique and some useful tips. It also gives the most common errors committed by candidates in the examination. Study these errors carefully, because you don't want to fall into the same traps. Make sure you avoid them in the exam!

The Speaking Test

Speak clearly and as slowly as you need to. You will not be given the benefit of the doubt if you mumble or speak inaudibly. If you realise you have just made a mistake, don't be afraid to go back and put it right, but don't make an issue of it. At the same time, don't think back all the time to what you have just said. This wastes time. Concentrate more on what you are actually saying and what you are going to say.

Role-play

If you do not know the German for a word or phrase you need, try to think of another English word or phrase like it which you can put into German. Do not translate the role-play directly, but put it into the German you have learnt. You must learn to think on your feet, especially if you are tackling a Higher Level situation where a snag may be introduced to which you must make a positive and constructive response.

The Reading Test

Answer the questions precisely. Make sure you have all the relevant details. If there is a mark scheme on your question paper, look at it carefully as it will give you a good idea of how much information is required. Do not add irrelevant information. There is sometimes more material provided than you need for your answers. For example, you may be presented with a whole document, such as a menu, but the questions on it might cover only a small part of the material given. You must learn by practice to pick out as quickly as possible the material which the questions are aimed at. Don't panic if there are quite large sections of a document that you do not understand. There is a good chance the questions will not refer to those sections. Read the questions <u>before</u> you study the document and then you will find the relevant parts more quickly and not waste time trying to work out difficult bits which do not matter.

The Listening Test

During the gaps you will need to look ahead at the questions coming up, so that you already have a good idea of what you are about to hear. Do not jump to over-hasty conclusions about words which sound alike, e.g. do not confuse *suchen* with *versuchen* or *besuchen*, *bringen* with *verbringen*.

The Writing Test

You will most certainly have to write at least one letter. It is therefore silly to spoil a good answer through not knowing the correct way to start and end informal and formal letters. Several informal letters are included in this book and these may be used for guidance. Do remember that all the words which mean 'you' and 'your' begin with capitals in letters (but <u>only</u> in letters) – for example, *Du*, *Dich*, *Dir*, *Dein*, *Ihr*, *Euch*, *Euer*. A formal letter is printed opposite to illustrate some of the conventions used in German.

Apart from letters, you will have to write short messages, perhaps a shopping list, a postcard, a short note explaining where you have gone, a short description, a set of instructions.

Finally, there is the most demanding written exercise, an account, which may be a story or an article for a magazine or a newspaper. You

Writing Test

KEIMER VERLAG
BAD HONNEF

Schofield & Sims Ltd
Publishers
Herrn Jack Brierley
Dogley Mill
Fenay Bridge

Huddersfield HD8 ONQ
Großbritannien

Sehr geehrter Herr Brierley! 24. Juli 1987 I/s

Besten Dank für Ihren Brief vom 26. Juni 1987
und für die 3 Muster-Bücher.

Die letzten Muster-Bücher von Ihnen haben wir
in einer 1/2 Seiten - Anzeige in der Zeitschrift

        Praxis
        des neusprachlichen Unterrichts

angezeigt. Wir senden Ihnen anliegend ein
Beleg-Exemplar der PRAXIS zu. Die PRAXIS hat
eine Auflage von 9.000 Exemplaren und wird von
allen 23.000 Englisch-Lehrern an den 3.000
Gymnasien in Deutschland gelesen.

Die Reaktion auf die Anzeige war völlig negativ,
nämlich Null Anfragen auf Prüfstücke.

Wir möchten im Augenblick von weiteren Aktionen
für Ihre Titel absehen und kommen auf der
Frankfurter Buchmesse in diesem Herbst wieder
auf Sie zu.

Mit freundlichen Grüßen

E. Keimer Verlag

U. Polscher
U. Polscher

Rheingoldweg 4   Volksbank Siebengebirge
534 Bad Honnef   Konto-Nr. 5208
Postfach 1463   Postscheckkonto Köln
Tel. (02224) 5407   Nr. 296047-503

will probably be provided with stimulus material – pictures, a poster, an extract from a brochure, magazine or newspaper – or simply with a situation and points to be covered in your answer. The main difficulty which examination candidates have in answering this question stems from the deliberately vague terms in which it may be set. You may be given a fairly wide choice in the subject matter and asked to comment on four or five items. Do not be tempted to write too much, but do make sure you cover all the points. It is a good idea to divide your answer into as many paragraphs as there are points to be covered. This acts as a check and reminder of how much you have already written and how many points you still need to cover.

To gain a high mark for this answer, you must aim at a more sophisticated level of language and style than in the other answers in the Writing Tests. For instance, you ought to be using subordinate clauses and descriptive adjectives in your sentences. You must also express opinions and attitudes as well as giving factual information. In Topic Unit 4, you will find a question which has been provided with both a Basic and a Higher Level answer so that you can compare the two levels. Answers at Higher Level also require a greater degree of accuracy than at Basic Level, and you must certainly try to leave yourself enough time to check your work.

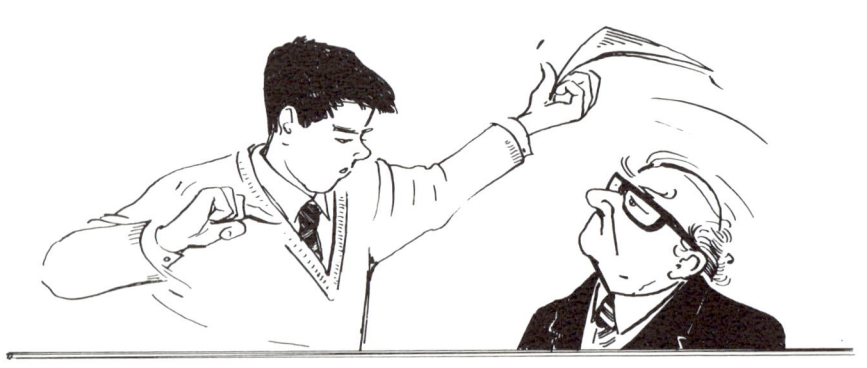

- Quantity is no substitute for quality!

Common Errors

Every year the examiners produce reports commenting, among other things, on the most common errors they have found in the examination answers. Here are some of these:

- German place-names. If the name of a well-known town or river has its own German spelling, do use it in the Writing Test, e.g. *Köln, München, der Rhein, die Mosel*.
- Confusion of *Uhr* and *Stunde*. *Uhr* is a clock, watch, or o'clock and has nothing to do with 'hour' in the sense of a period of sixty minutes. *Stunde* means hour or lesson.

    e.g. *Es ist zehn Uhr.*
    It is ten o'clock.
    Ich weiß nicht, wie spät es ist, weil ich keine Uhr habe.
    I don't know what time it is because I haven't got a watch.
    Sie wartete drei Stunden im Regen.
    She waited for three hours in the rain.
    Wir freuen uns nicht auf die Deutschstunde, weil wir eine Arbeit schreiben.
    We are not looking forward to the German lesson because we are having a test.

- Certain words are too often misspelt. Here are just a few examples which you are likely to have to use:

die Gesamtschule (-n)	comprehensive school
Deutsch(land)	German(y)
französisch	French
interessant	interesting
zurück	back
schlecht	bad
die Familie (-n)	family

- The plurals of common nouns which are frequently used in the plural, e.g. *Dorf, Dörfer; Wald, Wälder; Stadt, Städte; Hand, Hände; Haus, Häuser.*
- The words for 'friend(s)' cause confusion and should be carefully distinguished:
    der Freund (pl. *Freunde*) means friend (who happens to be male) or boy-friend.
    Freunde is the general word for friends, either all male or a mixture of male and female.
    die Freundin (pl. *Freundinnen*) means friend (who happens to be female) or girl-friend.
    Freundinnen refers to female friends only.

Common Errors

- Certain words are confused with other words and need to be carefully distinguished, for example:
  wie and *wir*
  wie = how, as, like
  wir = we
  also and *auch*
  also = therefore, so
  auch = too, as well, also
  gehen and *fahren*
  gehen = to go (in general terms), walk
  fahren = to travel, drive, go (on a journey),
    e.g. *Gehst du samstags zur Schule?*
    Do you go to school on Saturdays?
    Wir fahren nächste Woche nach Spanien.
    We are going to Spain next week.

- Word order in main clauses – see Word Order in Grammar section, page 104.
- Making verbs match their subject(s). This is a simple checking process.
- Verbs which go with *sein* in the Perfect Tense – see Verbs in Grammar section, pages 98-99.
- Use of *gefallen*. This is an impersonal verb and so can be used only with the third person (singular or plural). It is used to express the idea of liking, but actually means 'to please'. In English we say 'I like it', but in German this has to be turned round to: 'it is pleasing to me': *es gefällt mir*. If you want to say 'they like the house', you would say *das Haus gefällt ihnen* (literally: 'the house is pleasing to them').
- How are you? *Wie geht es dir/Wie geht es Ihnen*? This is an impersonal construction in German and can cause problems when you answer the question or adapt it to refer to other people. Literally the question means: How goes it with you? and must be answered in the same terms: (*Es geht mir/uns*) *sehr gut*. In answer

to the contraction: *Wie geht's?*, it is sufficient to say (*Sehr*) *gut, danke*, but if you are writing a letter and want to say you are keeping well, you must remember that you are actually saying: *Es geht mir* (*sehr*) *gut.* If you want to go on to say you hope your pen-friend and/or anyone else is well, you must keep the construction impersonal and say something along the lines of: *Mir geht es sehr gut. Hoffentlich geht es Dir und Deiner Familie auch gut* (remember the capitals!). I am very well. I hope you and your family are also well.
- *Besuchen* (to visit). This verb does NOT take the dative case!
Mein Brieffreund besucht mich.
My pen-friend is visiting me.

- *Bleiben* or *wohnen*? *Bleiben* means 'to stay', but if staying means living you must use *wohnen*.
e.g. *Wir haben in einem guten Hotel gewohnt.*
We stayed at a good hotel.
Bleiben should be used only in the sense of 'to remain', to spend time.
e.g. *Wir blieben drei Tage in Wien.*
We stayed in Vienna for three days.
- *ie* or *ei*. There is no rule, but do try to get them the right way round, especially in commonly used words such as: *liebe(r), schreiben, dein, zwei, drei, klein, Brief, liegen.*

Reading Tests

This chapter consists of Reading Tests at both Basic and Higher Level. Marks have been allocated to each question, just as they would be in the examination.

Basic Level Reading Test

Answer all the questions in English. You will find the answers on page 126.

1. Letztes Jahr wurden Kartoffeln, Fisch, Brot, Käse und Milch teurer. Eier, Schweinefleisch, Obst, Geflügel und Butter wurden billiger.
   a) Name FOUR items which became more expensive. (4)
   b) Name FOUR items which became cheaper. (4)

2. a) What is being offered beside the box which has been ticked? (2)
   b) What information has to be filled in on the coupon? (4)

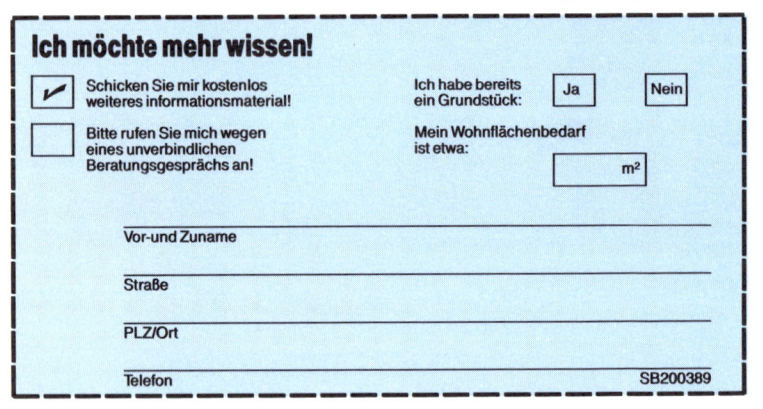

Ich möchte mehr wissen!

✓ Schicken Sie mir kostenlos weiteres informationsmaterial!

☐ Bitte rufen Sie mich wegen eines unverbindlichen Beratungsgesprächs an!

Ich habe bereits ein Grundstück: ☐ Ja ☐ Nein

Mein Wohnflächenbedarf ist etwa: ☐ m²

Vor-und Zuname

Straße

PLZ/Ort

Telefon   SB200389

3. a) What is on sale here? (1)
   b) Who are they intended for? (1)
   c) What is the main colour? (1)

5er-Pack Tennis-socken

Für die ganze Familie. Weiß mit farbigem Ringel. Baumwolle. Verschiedene Größen.

4. **Öffnungszeiten:**
   Täglich von 9.00 bis 18.00 Uhr. Nur für Fachbesucher. Kindern unter 10 Jahren ist der Zutritt nicht gestattet. Für sie steht eine vorbildlich eingerichtete Kindertagesstätte zur Verfügung.

   Which people are not allowed in? (1)

Basic Level Reading Test

5. Wer rastet, der rostet, und wer Sport treibt, bleibt fit. Man muß nicht gleich in einen der rund 100 Vereine gehen. Wie wär's zum Beispiel mit zehn Liegestützen jeden Morgen vor dem Frühstück?
   a) What must you do, according to this notice, to keep fit? (1)
   b) What are there about a hundred of in this town? (1)
   c) When does the notice suggest it is a good idea to do ten press-ups? (1)

6. The following information was given at the bottom of a restaurant menu. What does it tell you? (1)

   Übrigens: Alles auf der Speisekarte gibt es auch zum Mitnehmen.

7. # Fußball
   Samstagmittag um halb vier ist Bundesligazeit. Für zweimal 45 Minuten regiert König Fußball die Republik. Wenn die 18 Elite-Clubs um Meisterschaftspunkte kämpfen, treten alle anderen Sportarten in den Hintergrund. Und das schon seit 25 Jahren. Eine lange Zeit mit vielen Geschichten von Siegern und Verlierern, dramatischen und komischen Szenen.
   a) On which day and at what time do league football matches take place? (2)
   b) How long does a match last? (1)
   c) How long has there been a football league in Germany? (1)

8. Geöffnet haben wir für Sie jeden Montag bis Freitag von 9.00 bis 18.30. Samstags von 8.30 bis 14.00 Uhr und am langen Samstag sind wir von 8.30 bis 18.00 Uhr für Sie da.

   a) On which day(s) is this shop open from 9.00 a.m. until 6.30 p.m.? (1)
   b) How many extra hours does the shop stay open on the so-called 'long Saturday', compared with a normal Saturday? (1)

Basic Level Reading Test

9. Study the supermarket offers illustrated below and opposite, and then answer the questions at the foot of each page.

billig und nah

Holl. Speisekartoffeln
▷Bintje◁, mehligkochend, Klasse I
2,5 kg Beutel   **-.99**

Italienische Karotten
Klasse I
1000 g auf Foodtainer   **1.99**

Italienische Kiwi-Früchte
Stück   **-.49**

Italienische Tafeläpfel
▷Morgenduft◁, Klasse II
2 kg Tragetasche   **2.99**

Edelnelken
verschiedene Farben
jeder Strauß   **3.99**

Schokolade
verschiedene Sorten
100 g Tafel   **-.99**

Spanische Erdbeeren
Klasse I
sonnengereifte Früchte
250-g Schale   **1.79**

Belgischer Kopfsalat
Klasse I
große, schwere Köpfe
Stück   **-.79**

Französische Creme-Champignons
ein besonders würziger und aromatischer Speisepilz
1-kg   **4.99**

Spanischer Stangenspargel
Klasse I 16 m/m+
Das königliche Gemüse
500-g Bund   **5.99**

Part 1 a) Which TWO advantages are suggested to shoppers in the title billing? (2)
b) From which FIVE countries do some of the products come? (5)
c) Name FOUR vegetables on offer. (4)
d) Name THREE kinds of fruit on offer. (3)
e) Name ONE other product advertised here. (1)

116

Basic Level Reading Test

Erbsen sehr fein
mit oder ohne Möhren
oder junge, grüne
Bohnen fein, ganz.
je 850-ml-Dose

GARANTIERT **frisch**
Ital.
Äpfel
Golden Delicious, Klasse 2,
SB-verpackt
1 kg

Gehacktes
gemischt
Schwein+Rind
100 g

Original
Schwarzwälder
Schinken mild gesalzen
und aromatisch geräuchert
je 100 g

Aprikosen
geschält, 1/2 Frucht
Williams-Christ-Birnen
1/2 Frucht
Tortenpfirsiche in Scheiben
je 850-ml-Dose

Dauerwurst
Aufschnitt
Spitzenqualität
3 Sorten
je 100 g

Saftbockwurst
8 Stück = 720 g Abtropfgewicht.
in zarter Eigenhaut.
je Glas

Küchentücher
dick & durstig
4 Rollen

Part 2 a) Name TWO vegetables on offer. (2)
b) Name THREE kinds of fruit on offer. (3)
c) Name THREE meat products advertised here. (3)
d) Which product is described as 'thick and thirsty'? (1)

10. What change is advertised in Edinburgh from next May? (1)

> **Edinburgh – Rund um die Uhr**
> Ab Mai nächsten Jahres ist der Flughafen Edinburgh 24 Stunden täglich geöffnet.

11. Study this weather forecast and then answer the questions.

Reisewetter der nächsten drei Tage

Norddeutschland: Bewölkt mit Regen- und Graupelschauern. Temperaturen um sieben Grad. Donnerstag kälter.
Süddeutschland: Stark bewölkt, zeitweise Regen und Schnee. Höchsttemperaturen: vier bis sechs Grad.
Österreich-Schweiz: Bewölkt, zeitweise Schneefall, in den Tälern Regen. Im Süden heiter. Null bis 6 Grad.
Italien-Korsika-Balearen-Malta: Heiter bis wolkig. Zeitweise Regen. Im Süden bis 15 Grad.
Kanarische Inseln: Teils heiter, teils wolkig. Zeitweise Regen und Gewitter. 18 bis 22 Grad.

a) Where will the temperature reach four to six degrees Celsius at the most? (1)
b) What will Thursday be like in North Germany? (1)
c) Where may thunderstorms be expected? (1)
d) What kind of weather is forecast only for South Germany, Austria and Switzerland? (1)
e) Name one place where the weather might be wet and warm. (1)
f) For whom is this forecast intended and for how far ahead does it make a prediction? (2)

12. **Wenn der Frühling kommt, kommt auch bald die Reisezeit – und ein altes, aber immer wieder „heißes" Thema: Trampen ja oder nein. Trampen per Autostop ist bestimmt die billigste Art zu reisen – aber nicht immer die beste. Manchmal ist es ziemlich unbequem – zum Beispiel bei Nacht oder wenn es regnet. Und manchmal ist es auch gefährlich, besonders für Mädchen. Viele Eltern sind deshalb gegen das Trampen. Da gibt es dann zu Hause harte Diskussionen.**

The writer of this extract makes THREE points about hitch-hiking. What are they? (3)

13. **Haus Waldblick**

Skiwanderwoche
Den Urlaub in familiärer Umgebung genießen. Die gemütliche Hotel-Pension „Waldblick" bietet ihnen modern ausgestattete Zimmer mit Dusche/WC (auf Wunsch mit TV).
Morgens erwartet Sie ein großes Frühstücksbuffet. Unser Hotelbus fährt Sie täglich ins Skizentrum Ravensberg. Hier stehen Ihnen 3 Skilifte und 50 km gepflegte Loipen zur Verfügung.
Das 29 Grad warme Hallenbad ist nur wenige Minuten von unserem Haus entfernt. Einmal wöchentlich fahren wir zur Wildfütterung.

Gesamtpreis bei 7 Übernachtungen:
mit Frühstück = DM 275,00
mit Halbpens. = DM 365,00   je Person
mit Vollpens. = DM 435,00   ohne Kurbeitrag

Im Preis eingeschlossen:
Zimmer mit Dusche/WC, Begrüßungsgetränk, Wildfütterung, einmal Hallenbad, tägl. Busservice zum Skizentrum und Verleih von Langlaufski.

Buchungen für 2-25 Personen möglich.

a) How can hotel guests get to the skiing centre? (1)
b) What facilities are available for swimmers? (2)
c) What would one person have to pay for a week's stay with bed and breakfast? (1)

Higher Level Reading Test

Answer all the questions in English. You will find the answers on pages 126 and 127.

1. A department store makes the following claim:

    ALLES UNTER EINEM DACH

    What is its claim? (1)

2. What is for sale here and what are they made of? (2)

    Damenschultertaschen
    Aus echtem Leder.
    Verschiedene Modelle.
    In Schwarz, Braun oder Blau.

3. Which FOUR departments are offering sale goods? (4)

*Winterschlußverkauf vom 30.1-11.2.
nur in unseren Abteilungen Textilien,
Schuhe, Lederwaren und Bettwaren.*

4. Name FOUR items on Berlin's programme for the autumn and winter months of 1988. (4)

Berlin, die ,,Kulturstadt Europas 1988" bietet allen Besuchern auch im Herbst und im Winter ein umfangreiches Programm. Ausstellungen, Weihnachtsmärkte, Konzerte und große Sportereignisse sind die Stichworte für die kalte Jahreszeit. Alle wichtigen Informationen enthält die neueste Ausgabe der Veranstaltungsübersicht ,,Berlin tut gut".

5.
In Köln.
Mit Blick auf den weltberühmten Dom,
finden Sie perfekten Service
und traditionelle deutsche Gastlichkeit.

This is part of an advertisement for a hotel. Where is the hotel and what view do you get from it? (2)

6.
Alle wichtigen Sehenswürdigkeiten sind im Stadtzentrum leicht zu Fuß zu erreichen. Der Fahrpreis für die öffentlichen Verkehrsmittel beträgt 20 Pfennig.

a) What claim is made for the sights of this town? (1)
b) What costs 20 pfennigs? (1)

7. Study this notice about theatre performances.

● **Vorstellungsbeginn Dienstag, 20.12.,** 20 Uhr (Premiere) ● **Wochentags:** 15.30 und 20.00 Uhr ● **1. und 2. Weihnachtsfeiertag:** Jeweils 11.00, 15.00 und 19.00 Uhr ● **Silvester:** 15.00 und 19.00 Uhr ● **Heiligabend** keine Vorstellung

a) How many performances are there on a weekday? (1)
b) When are there three performances? (1)
c) When is there no performance? (1)
d) What is the programme for New Year's Eve? (1)

Higher Level Reading Test

8. **Ferienwohnungen ...**

Aus unserem umfangreichen Angebot einige Beispiele:

A) Wohn-Schlafzimmer mit Küche, 2 Betten,
Dusche/WC und TV
DM 35,00 pro Tag
zuzüglich DM 25,00 Endreinigung

B) Wohnzimmer, Schlafzimmer, Küche,
Bad/WC, 3 Betten
DM 40,00 pro Tag für 2 Personen
DM 7,50 für die 3. Person,
zuzüglich Endreinigung DM 35,00,
Nebenkosten für Strom, Heizung, Handtücher.

C) Appartement mit Wohnzimmer, Schlafzimmer,
Küche, Bad/WC, TV, Fitnessräumen, 2 Betten und
Doppelschlafcouch.
DM 45,00 bis 100,00 pro Tag
zuzüglich Endreinigung DM 40,00.

a) In what ways is holiday flat B superior to holiday flat A? (3)
b) Name TWO things which are charged as extras in holiday flat B. (2)
c) For how many people is sleeping accommodation provided in flat C? (1)

9. Read the following article about the West German football league and then answer the questions on page 122.

Die Zeiten und Zahlen ändern sich

24. August 1963. In acht Stadien zwischen Bremen und München wird ein neues Zeitalter angepfiffen: die Fußball-Bundesliga. Sie entwickelt sich schnell. Das beweisen die Zahlen. 1200 Mark Gehalt, 250 Mark für ein gewonnenes Spiel, 3000 Mark für die Meisterschaft: das sind die finanziellen Daten aus dem Gründungsjahr. Ein Spieler konnte also pro Saison zwischen 25 000 und 35 000 Mark verdienen. Diese Gage wird heute im Monat gezahlt. Bei den Ablösesummen – wenn ein Verein einen Spieler „verkauft" – ist das nicht anders. 1963 war die Höchstsumme noch 25 000 Mark. 1984 kassierte Bayern München für den Transfer von Stürmerstar Karl-Heinz Rummenigge zu Inter Mailand 11,2 Millionen Mark. Auch in der Bundesliga wird heute über die früheren Ablösesummen gelacht. Ein neuer Rekord wurde im letzten Sommer aufgestellt. Der VfB Stuttgart bezahlte für Mauricio Gaudino – er spielte für Waldhof Mannheim – 2,4 Millionen Mark.

a) How many teams took part in the first football league matches on 24th August 1963? (1)
b) How much bonus was paid in those days for a victory on the football field? (1)
c) What, according to the article, is meant by an „*Ablösesumme*"? (2)
d) Can you find the German word for Milan? (1)
e) What kind of a record was set in the summer of 1987? (2)

10. *Advent, Advent*

Nicht nur Heiligabend und die beiden Feiertage, sondern schon die Wochen vorher gehören zu Weihnachten. Immer früher beginnt in den Geschäften das große Weihnachtsgeschäft. Die Hauptgeschäftsstraßen in den Städten werden prachtvoll geschmückt. Auf den großen Plätzen werden hohe Tannenbäume aufgestellt. Am 1. Dezember bekommen alle Kinder in unserer Familie einen Adventskalender mit 24 Fenstern. Man macht an jedem Tag ein Fenster auf. So weiß man immer, wie lange es noch bis Heiligabend ist.
Erst am Abend vor Heiligabend stellen wir den Weihnachtsbaum ins Wohnzimmer. Wir schmücken ihn mit roten Äpfeln, Plätzchen, Strohsternen und kleinen Figuren aus Holz. Viele Leute nehmen heute schon elektrische Kerzen. Wir stecken weiße Wachskerzen auf die grünen Zweige. Das sieht schöner aus. Zur Bescherung an Heiligabend brennen die Kerzen dann zum erstenmal. So wird dies zu einem besonderem Ereignis. Wir singen Weihnachtslieder, und jeder von uns Kindern darf ein Weihnachtsgedicht vortragen. Dann gibt es die Geschenke.
Am ersten Feiertag gibt es als Festessen meistens eine Weihnachtsgans. Am zweiten Feiertag besuchen wir dann Freunde und Verwandte.
                                        Norbert (13 Jahre)

a) What point does the author make about Christmas shopping? (1)
b) What are to be seen at this time in town squares? (1)
c) What do you do with an advent calendar? (1)
d) When does this family bring the Christmas tree into the living-room? (1)
e) Name THREE Christmas-tree decorations mentioned here. (3)
f) When are the candles lit for the first time? (1)
g) On this special occasion, what is each child allowed to do?
h) What does the family do on Boxing Day? (1)

11. Read the passage on the next page about housing problems in Germany and then answer the questions which follow.

In den Städten herrscht Wohnungsnot. Etwa zwei Millionen Mietwohnungen fehlen. In den Hochhäusern können viele Menschen wohnen, aber Hochhäuser haben Nachteile. Ärzte sagen, daß Kinder dort nicht gesund aufwachsen. Viele kleine Kinder haben Angst, wenn sie aus dem Fenster schauen. Sie kennen nur den Fahrstuhl und keine Treppen. Sie sind oft zu klein, um allein im Fahrstuhl zu fahren. Und wenn sie auf dem Spielplatz sind, können die Mütter sie nicht vom Fenster aus beobachten. Viele Erwachsene denken, das Kinderzimmer ist unwichtig. Deshalb ist es oft der kleinste Raum in der Wohnung mit den billigsten Möbeln. Kinder, die auf dem Land oder in kleinen Städten wohnen, haben es besser. Sie haben mehr Platz zum Spielen, und sie sind nicht so oft krank wie die Großstadt-Kinder.

a) How many rented flats are needed? (1)
b) What do doctors say about children living in high-rise blocks? (2)
c) List THREE difficulties mentioned in connection with small children. (6)
d) What does the article say about the children's room? (3)
e) Why are children who live in the country or small towns better off than those living in cities? (2)

12. Service am Bahnhof

Bevor ihre Urlaubsreise startet, sollten Sie sich noch ein bißchen Zeit nehmen, um zu entdecken, was Ihnen ein Bahnhof so alles bietet.
Dort haben Sie nämlich auch am späten Abend sowie an Sonn- und Feiertagen noch eine Vielzahl von Einkaufsmöglichkeiten. Ein Buch oder eine Zeitung für die Reise vielleicht, Spielzeug für die aufgeregten Kleinen oder auch eine Wurst oder ein Bier gegen das Reisefieber. Wenn Sie mehr Zeit haben, können Sie auch zu einem ausgiebigen Menü Platz nehmen.
Wenn Sie feststellen, daß Sie vergessen haben, Geld abzuheben oder Devisen zu tauschen, ist auch das schnell erledigt. An 36 großen Bahnhöfen können Sie bis in die Abendstunden Geld wechseln, mit Eurocheques abheben oder in Devisen umtauschen.
Und bei Ihrer Rückkehr finden Sie auf dem Bahnhof alles, was Sie brauchen, um den heimischen Kühlschrank wieder aufzufüllen.

a) When can you shop at a German station outside normal business hours? (3)
b) Give FIVE examples of items on sale. (5)
c) What kind of financial transactions can you make at 36 large stations? (3)
d) What kind of useful shopping might you do for yourself on a homeward journey? (1)

Basic Level Listening Test

Listening Tests

Switch on the cassette and find the Listening Tests section near the end of Side 2. You will hear a brief introduction, followed first of all by the material for the Basic Level Test.

Basic Level Listening Test

Listen to each item in turn and then answer the following questions in English. You will find the answers on pages 127 and 128.

1. Where does the speaker come from?
2. How often does a disco take place?
3. What task needs to be done?
4. What is the speaker's problem?
5. What does the questioner want to know?
6. When does the next performance begin?
7. What is the customer buying?
8. Where is the chemist's shop?
9. What does the speaker want to know?
10. a) How many brothers and sisters has the speaker got?
    b) How are the brother and sisters identified?
11. Why is the customer buying a record?
12. a) How does Dagmar get to school?
    b) How long does it take her?
    c) At what time does school begin?
    d) How many lessons are there on Saturdays?
    e) What happens on Thursday afternoons?
    f) What happens on the other afternoons?
13. a) What was Peter doing in the park?
    b) Where did he put his anorak?
    c) Why did Peter leave that part of the park?
    d) At what time did he look for his anorak?
    e) Give FOUR details about the anorak.
14. a) Where does Vera work?
    b) How often does she work there?
    c) What time does she get up for work?
15. a) What sort of flowers are mentioned?
    b) Give THREE facts about the flower shop.
16. a) What sort of ticket is the passenger buying?
    b) What time is the next train?
    c) What facility is mentioned in connection with this train?

17. a) How do you get to the market-place?
    b) How can the first speaker find out where the *Winzerstraße* is?

Higher Level Listening Test

Now do the Higher Level Test. Listen to each item in turn and then answer the following questions in English. You will find the answers on page 128.

1. Why was no one in the office?
2. When can the speaker not sleep?
3. a) At what age can you drive a moped in Germany?
   b) Why do many young people in Germany buy a moped as soon as they can?
4. a) What is the busiest time?
   b) Where else does Vera work?
5. When would the dentist like to see his patient again?
6. a) Where is Gerhard?
   b) What is there for lunch apart from meatballs?
   c) Name FIVE ingredients of the meatballs.
7. a) Give FOUR details about the bag.
   b) Name SEVEN different items in it.
8. a) How long has the boy been playing chess?
   b) When does he play chess at school?
   c) On what day and at what time does the chess club meet?
9. Which FOUR tasks has Frau Kunert performed in the kitchen?
10. a) When was Dorle to get her brother's room?
    b) What extra piece of furniture does Dorle need in the room?
    c) Why is Dorle's mother happy to get rid of the wardrobe and chest of drawers?
    d) How does her mother plan to replace the furniture?
11. a) What is the boy allergic to?
    b) How is the problem solved?
12. a) What symptoms does the patient have?
    b) What does the doctor claim the cough syrup will do, apart from ease the cough?
    c) Why is the patient anxious to get well as soon as possible?

Answers

Answers to Basic Level Reading Test

1. a) 4 of: potatoes, fish, bread, cheese, milk b) 4 of: eggs, pork, fruit, poultry, butter
2. a) further information free of charge b) first name, surname, address, telephone number
3. a) tennis socks b) the whole family c) white
4. children below 10 years of age
5. a) sport b) clubs c) every morning before breakfast
6. everything on the menu is available as takeaway food
7. a) Saturday at 3.30 p.m. b) 90 minutes c) 25 years
8. a) Monday to Friday b) 4 hours
9. *Part 1* a) cheap and nearby
    b) Holland, Italy, Spain, Belgium, France
    c) 4 of: potatoes, carrots, lettuce, mushrooms, asparagus
    d) kiwi fruit, apples, strawberries
    e) chocolate
   Part 2 a) peas, beans
    b) 3 of: apples, pears, apricots, peaches
    c) 3 of: mince, sausage, ham, sliced cold meat
    d) kitchen towels
10. the airport will be open 24 hours a day
11. a) South Germany b) colder c) Canary Islands d) snow e) 1 of: Canary Islands, Malta, Italy, Corsica, Balearics f) travellers/holiday-makers; 3 days
12. it is the cheapest form of travel; it can be rather uncomfortable; it is sometimes dangerous
13. a) on the hotel bus b) there is a heated indoor pool a few minutes from the hotel c) 275 marks

Answers to Higher Level Reading Test

1. everything is under one roof
2. ladies' shoulder-bags made of leather
3. textiles, shoes, leather goods, bedding
4. exhibitions, Christmas markets, concerts, sporting events
5. it is in Cologne; the view is of the world-famous cathedral
6. a) all important sights are easily accessible on foot in town centre
    b) the fare for public transport

Answers: Basic Level Listening Test

7. a) 2 b) Christmas Day and Boxing Day c) Christmas Eve d) 2 performances, at 3.00 p.m. and 7.00 p.m.
8. a) it has a separate bedroom; it has a bath; it has 3 beds b) 2 of: electricity, heating, towels c) 4
9. a) 16 b) 250 marks c) the sum involved when a club sells a player d) *Mailand* e) a Stuttgart club paid the record sum of 2.4 million marks for a player
10. a) it begins earlier every year b) tall Christmas trees c) you open a window every day d) the evening before Christmas Eve e) 3 of: red apples, biscuits, straw stars, little wooden figures, candles f) at the distribution of presents on Christmas Eve g) to recite a Christmas poem h) they visit friends and relations
11. a) 2 million b) they do not grow up healthy c) 3 of: they are afraid when they look out of the window; they only know lifts and not stairs; they are often too small to use lifts on their own; their mothers cannot see them when they are out playing d) many adults think it is unimportant; it is often the smallest room in the flat; it often has the cheapest furniture e) they have more space to play in and are not ill as often as town children
12. a) late evening, Sundays, public holidays b) books, newspapers, toys, sausage, beer c) change money, cash eurocheques, change to and from foreign currency d) you can shop to refill your fridge

Answers to Basic Level Listening Test

1. Austria
2. once a month
3. laying the table
4. he cannot hear anything
5. where he can buy chocolate
6. at half-past four
7. petrol or diesel
8. in the town centre
9. where he can best park
10. a) 3 b) brother has red hair; sisters have long blonde hair
11. for her son's birthday
12. a) by bus b) half an hour c) ten-past eight d) 4 e) sport f) they are free
13. a) playing football with his friends b) on a bench c) to go to an ice-cream kiosk d) about 11 o'clock e) 4 of: pale grey; dark blue collar; zip at front; lots of pockets; thick; warm

Answers: Higher Level Listening Test

14. a) on the market b) 3 times a week c) 5 o'clock
15. a) roses b) 3 of: round the corner; between supermarket and bank; flowers not too expensive; only flower shop in town.
16. a) second-class return b) 10.33 c) dining-car
17. a) go to next set of traffic-lights and turn left b) by looking at town plan in the market-place

Answers to Higher Level Listening Test

1. it was too late
2. when he cannot hear traffic
3. a) 15 b) to be independent
4. a) noon b) in the theatre
5. in 2 weeks
6. a) having a guitar lesson b) potatoes and cauliflower c) 5 of: minced meat, onion, breadcrumbs, egg, pepper, salt
7. a) quite small, about half a meter long, made of brown leather, quite old. b) 7 of: Thermos flask, paperbacks, newspaper, apple, bar of chocolate, playing-cards, blue jumper, street plan of Cologne
8. a) 3 years b) in the lunch-break c) alternate Fridays between 6 and 10 p.m.
9. washed up breakfast things, cleaned floor, peeled potatoes and washed lettuce
10. a) when he got married b) a writing desk c) they are old-fashioned and heavy d) Dorle's father will make built-in furniture
11. a) pork b) he will eat an egg dish
12. a) sore throat and can hardly speak b) help her sleep c) she is a teacher and needs her voice for work